Talking About Stepfamilies

Other Bradbury Books by Maxine B. Rosenberg

*Not My Family: Sharing the Truth
About Alcoholism*

Growing Up Adopted

TALKING ABOUT STEPFAMILIES

Maxine B. Rosenberg

Afterword by Emily Visher,
cofounder, Stepfamily Association of America

Bradbury Press New York
Collier Macmillan Canada Toronto
Maxwell Macmillan International Publishing Group
New York Oxford Singapore Sydney

Bradbury Press
Macmillan Publishing Company
866 Third Avenue
New York, NY 10022

Collier Macmillan Canada, Inc.
1200 Eglinton Avenue East
Suite 200
Don Mills, Ontario M3C 3N1

Printed and bound in the United States of America

First Edition

10 9 8 7 6 5 4 3 2 1

All photographs in this book
were taken by Maxine B. Rosenberg,
except for the pictures on pages
18, 26, 42, 78, and 98, which were provided
by the subjects' families.

Book design by Michael Ian Kaye

Library of Congress Cataloging-in-Publication Data
Rosenberg, Maxine B.
Talking about stepfamilies / by
Maxine B. Rosenberg. — 1st ed.
p. cm.
Includes bibliographical references.
Summary: Children and adults
who have become part of stepfamilies
describe their experiences in coping with
new stepparents and stepsiblings.
ISBN 0-02-777913-0
1. Stepchildren—United States—Psychology—Case
studies—Juvenile literature.
2. Stepfamilies—United States—Case studies—
Juvenile literature. 3. Stepchildren—United
States—Family relationships—Case
studies—Juvenile literature.
[1. Stepchildren. 2. Stepfamilies.] I. Title.
HQ777.7.R675 1990 306.874—dc20 90-33540 CIP AC

Acknowledgments

I would like to give special thanks to the following people who made this book possible: the stepchildren and their families who generously gave me their time; my children Karin and Seth, who trusted me to interview their friends; my editor, Sharon Steinhoff, for her constant encouragement; and my husband, Paul, for his patience, understanding, and interest in the project.

To Edna, my stepmom—
who's added more spice
to the family

Contents

Contents

. . . .

Talking About Stepfamilies

Author's Note

Twelve years ago, my mother died. One year later, my father remarried. Although I was married myself by then and had four children, I still was angry and hurt that another woman was taking my mom's place. While I liked my stepmother and appreciated my father's need for a companion, I was hesitant about getting close to a stranger who was suddenly a part of my life.

Interviewing the stepchildren for this book was generally a me-too experience, though there were some surprises. Particularly fascinating were the different emphases in the stories of stepsiblings: what was uppermost in one child's mind was not necessarily a big issue for the other. For instance, Douglas's major concern was his joint custody arrangement, while his stepbrother Owen focused on his relationship with his stepfather. Siblings in the same

1

family, upon becoming stepchildren, also often reacted differently to similar situations.

Making a stepfamily work is not easy for anyone. It takes at least two years from the time of the remarriage for adults and children to adjust to one another's personalities. Since stepfamilies are founded on loss—either through divorce or death—both the adults and children must mourn the passing of the old family before they can accept the new one. In the case of children, a stepfamily may mean new siblings as well as a new parent. Furthermore, children who've lived through divorce must let go of the fantasy that their parents will someday reunite.

When young people become part of a stepfamily, more than relationships change. Children may have to switch schools, leave friends, or alternate houses as part of a custody arrangement. All of these difficulties can be overcome. But, as the stories in this book make clear, adjustments take time, along with patience, determination, and hard work. This is not to say, however, that *all* stepfamilies resolve their problems.

Unlike my other books, for which it took a while to find suitable subjects, I had no difficulty locating stepchildren, young and old. Friends, neighbors, my children, school nurses, social workers—all thought of someone who might want to share his or her story with me. Looking at the available statistics, this comes as no surprise.

According to 1987 United States Census Bureau figures, there are 4.3 million stepfamilies in this country, with approximately 1300 new ones formed each day. These families include 8.7 million children under the age of eighteen. More simply, one out of five minors is a stepchild. The Stepfamily Association of America cites demographers' predictions that by the turn of the century, the stepfamily will be the most common family configuration in America.

Prior to World War II, most stepfamilies came into being when a parent died. At that time, divorce was something to be avoided as well as kept secret. After the war, though, it became more acceptable. Marital breakups steadily increased, until by 1977, 50 percent of all marriages ended in divorce.

Interestingly, while the younger stepchildren I spoke to live in an age when divorce and stepfamilies are more common, they still view their families as different from the norm. Children often told me that they felt particularly isolated—"odd," "weird," and "strange"—the first year or two following a parent's remarriage. Like stepchildren in the past, they too tried to hide their family situation. Fortunately, today, with more resources available for support (family support groups, school counseling groups, and therapists), stepchildren and their families can get help during rough times.

Despite difficult adjustments, the stepchildren I spoke to felt they grew in many ways from their stepfamily experience. For one, they became more flexible as they changed homes, followed different sets of rules, and learned to adapt to a variety of personalities. Furthermore, they became wise, at an early age, about the dynamics of marriage and adult relationships. And they began thinking,

quite young, about the importance of family. All the children looked forward to marriage, but those who had lived
through divorce worried about repeating their parents' mistakes. Every stepchild intended to marry just once—that
marriage would be forever—yet without hesitating, these
same stepchildren said that constant arguing between husband and wife would mean the marriage had to end.

To ensure a diverse group of people for this book, I interviewed many more subjects than space would allow me
to include. When stories overlapped or repeated themes, I
chose the strongest. I intentionally included only stories
from stepchildren who, along with their parents and stepparents, have tried hard to make their blended family succeed (perhaps after some initial resistance). These positive
stories, I felt, offered the most constructive advice to families in similar situations.

Each interview was tape recorded in the subject's home,
with younger children talking about an hour, while adults
spoke for more than two. Later on, there were many back
and forth phone calls to go over information, clarify issues,
and check facts.

Except for one child, no names have been changed. A
young boy first thought he'd use a pseudonym, then later
decided not to. "Let my parents know how I feel," he said.
Some interviewees felt comfortable having me photograph
them, others wanted to supply their own photographs, and
some, to protect the privacy of other family members, chose
to have no photos included at all.

Most of the children seemed to enjoy the experience of

being interviewed. When I finished talking to one girl, she asked if I'd like to speak to her friend, also a stepchild. Then, on the spot, she phoned the girl. "Do it! It's fun," she exclaimed. Later on, the friend described her own interview as "awesome."

Adults too were happy after the interviews. More than one said, "It feels so good to talk." A parent—the mother and stepmother of two of the young interviewees—phoned me one day. "I'm glad my kids had the opportunity to speak to you," she said. "Now they seem more open to suggestions of going to family counseling, which I've wanted for so long."

In the end, as with all my other books, I grew from listening to people share their life experiences. What seems to ring true for all stepchildren, myself included, is that trusting new family members does not happen overnight. Rather, these feelings evolve over years with everyone working hard to make the stepfamily succeed.

Looking at my own family, I see that my life has been enhanced since my father's remarriage. Only yesterday, on the telephone, one of my stepsisters and I exchanged news of our joys and difficulties. We confided in each other as if we were biological sisters.

As for my stepmom and me, we're friends. The one particular thing that made our relationship work is that she never tried to be my mother. Nor did she ever say anything negative about my mom. From the beginning, she welcomed me into the home she shared with my dad. And slowly, the two of us came to know and accept each other.

Even better, we discovered we shared many interests.

Like every stepchild I interviewed, I too wish I could always have had my original family. But since that couldn't be, at least I have the best of all possible worlds.

Maxine B. Rosenberg
January 1990

KAREN AGE 10 ½

"I had the jitters before the remarriage"

"For as long as I can remember, my parents have been divorced and Mom has worked full-time. Mom and I lived together for eight years in a three-room, cramped, basement apartment. Then nine months ago, she remarried. Now Mom and Joe, my stepfather, and I live in a big house with my animals, two cats and a dog. Finally I have my own room, which Joe painted exactly the way I like."

Ever since her parents' separation, Karen has seen her father every Thursday and every other weekend. "Dad's house isn't that far away. Usually when I visit him, we take walks along the aqueduct, or we explore the woods. Of all the people I know, Dad's the one I have the most fun with. I like being with Mom, too, but when she and I are together, we mostly talk.

"About two years ago, I noticed that Mom seemed lonely.

Before meeting Joe, she used to spend a lot of time with my aunt—her sister—who was also single. The two of them confided in each other and enjoyed doing things together. Then my aunt got married, and Mom was the only single person left in the family. Although she had lots of boy-friends, she never found anyone she could settle down with. That was good in a way because none of those men really seemed interested in me. They'd act nice enough in front of Mom to impress her, but I could tell they weren't sincere.

"So when Mom's friend suggested she go out with this nice man who had never been married before, Mom said okay. That man was Joe, and from the start Mom liked him."

After dating Joe for five months, Karen's mother introduced him to her. "Mom wanted to get to know him first, which was wise. As it turned out, I too liked him right away, and soon the three of us started going places together on weekends. When Joe and I felt more comfortable with each other, he offered to take my friends and me out for the day if Mom had to work. Once he took us ice-skating, another time to an amusement park. I thought he was nice to do that, and so did Mom.

"That's why I wasn't surprised when she told me they were getting married. By then we three did so much to-gether, I kind of expected it."

Karen's glad her mother worked hard to make sure she and Joe got along well before he became her stepfather. "Not only were Joe and I with each other a lot before the marriage, but Mom and I talked many times about what

. . . .

having a stepparent might be like. While I knew Mom and I would still be close, I wondered how she'd make decisions once she remarried. Since Mom wasn't that strict—her worst punishment was sending me to my room—I worried that, with Joe, she might change her ways.

"When I told her how I felt, she promised that those kind of things would stay the same. Luckily I have the kind of mother who listens to me. It's important for parents and kids to tell one another their feelings, especially if they're in a stepfamily. I owe it to Mom for making it easier between Joe and me. And Joe also tried hard.

"Still, I had the jitters before the remarriage."

To complicate matters, it seemed likely that, with Joe in the family, they would move to a larger house, maybe in another town. "One part of me was excited about Mom's remarriage—especially when she said I could invite my friends to the wedding. Yet, another part of me felt scared, not knowing what would happen next. It was a confusing time.

"Mostly I worried about not seeing my father as often. And I didn't want to change schools, since I had always done well in my classes and was even in the honors program. Also, I liked my neighborhood and had lots of friends there. The last thing I wanted to do was say good-bye to everyone."

Much to Karen's surprise, the remarriage and the move had fewer rough spots than she had expected. "In May, soon after the wedding, we moved to a bigger house in the next town. When I started fifth grade in the fall, it was hard not knowing any of the kids, but I was determined to meet people. I thought, If I sit like a little shy girl, waiting for someone to come over to me, I'll end up all by myself. Instead I said, 'Take a deep breath and don't be a scaredy cat.' Then I went right up to the kids. Now I have more friends than I ever had, and some are really nice. And I still live close enough to my old friends to see them on weekends and holidays. Dad isn't far away either, and I visit him the same amount as always."

While Karen was getting used to her new school, she also had to get accustomed to being with Joe, sometimes without her mother around. "Since Joe's a teacher, he's usually home when I get off the school bus. Once in a while he has a meeting to go to, and then he comes in a little later. Mom, who's a social worker, gets home at five-thirty.

"Right away I was glad not to have to come home to a baby-sitter anymore. Still, in the beginning, I felt uncomfortable. I'd come through the door and Joe would say, 'What'd you do in school today?' I'd answer, 'Nothing much.' Then, to be polite, I'd ask him how his work went, and he'd reply, 'Fine.'

"Now that we've lived together awhile and know each other better, I confide in Joe when things are bothering me. If my friend Stephanie and I have an argument, for instance, I'll talk about it with him, and he listens. A few days later, he'll ask me if everything's okay, which makes me feel he's really interested. The best part about Joe is that he's never too nosy."

Although Karen likes Joe, she hasn't forgotten her father.

. . . .

"I love being with Dad and know we will always have fun together. Last summer he and I went camping, and this year we're planning a trip to California. Even when I only go to his house, I totally relax. There, I just have to feed his dog and, once in a while, clean up the dishes. Visiting him is like being on vacation. At home, I have many more responsibilities: doing my own laundry, straightening my room, taking care of the animals, and cleaning the dishes. No wonder being with Dad is a treat!

"Dad knows I look forward to seeing him, but since the remarriage, I sense that he's jealous of Joe. I think he worries that I might like Joe more than him. He'll ask, 'Is Joe treating you right?' Maybe Dad wants to make sure *he* will always be my dad, and no one will take his place. It probably would be easier if Dad was married, too."

Four and a half years ago, Karen's father did remarry, but the marriage only lasted a year and a half. "I was six when Dad married Cathy, and although she wasn't his wife for that long, I got attached to her. Every time I saw her, she was happy: smiling, singing, and laughing. Cathy made it even more special at Dad's. Then one weekend she wasn't there. When Dad said she wouldn't be coming back, I was completely shocked. Why would Cathy leave without saying good-bye to me? I felt like I had lost someone close.

"About six months later, she called my house and asked me to lunch. I said yes, but for some reason, I didn't have a good time when we went out. I guess I was still too angry at her for what she had done."

Cathy has continued to call Karen and invite her to the

movies or to a restaurant. Now Karen no longer feels as comfortable being with her and says she probably won't accept the next invitation. "These are the things about divorce and being a stepchild that make it so hard. You get close to someone, and then they're gone. I don't think most people understand how frightening that is for a kid. So many times I meet adults who tell me how lucky I am to have two dads and a mother who are caring. As far as that goes, I agree with them. Still, people don't realize that even though I was so young when my parents divorced, it hasn't been easy for me."

Since Joe has become part of her family, Karen has also discovered that her relationship with her mother has changed. "I used to be the one to hear about things that upset Mom. She treated me more like an adult than her young daughter. In a way, I was her friend. Now Mom tells Joe all her secrets, and I feel left out. That's not to say Mom and I aren't close. If I have a problem, she's the one I go to. Joe doesn't like it when I insist on talking to Mom alone. I don't know why he takes it personally. I like him, but sometimes I need to have Mom to myself.

"Yet Joe's more lenient than Mom, and sometimes he sees things more from my point of view. The other day, Mom said I couldn't walk to the shopping center with my friends, but Joe convinced her to let me go. If the decision isn't that serious, Mom gives in.

"For a long time, I hoped Mom and Dad would get back together, since I love both of them so much. There was a time I even blamed myself for their troubles. Finally, though, I understand that they weren't right for each other. Maybe talking to other stepchildren in a group at school helped me to see that."

Today Karen has a new wish—to have a brother or sister. With two adults in the house again, she is more aware of being an only child. "It's lonely for me as the only kid in the family. You'd think that because Joe has no children, he and Mom might want a child together, but so far they've not made any promises to me. At least if I had a sister or brother, there'd be someone in the house for me to turn to, especially when I'm mad at Mom or Joe. While I have friends to confide in, it's not the same. And all my cousins are much younger than I. Too bad Joe doesn't have children. It would have been nice having a stepbrother or -sister. One day I'm going to get married and have kids. I think it's exciting to bring children into this world.

"Right now, as a substitute, I have my cats and dog. When I feel low, I cuddle up with them. They're number one for comforting. I tell them my problems, and they just listen and understand me. We never disagree."

As her new family approaches its first anniversary, Karen is most proud of her own determination to make things work. "I'm glad I'm not the kind of kid who says, 'My mom's getting married. That's the end of everything.' With all the changes I had to make, I've still managed to keep up with my old friends, make new ones, have lots of hobbies— gymnastics, art, creative writing—and get good grades. In my new school I'm also in the honors program.

"In fact, the best part of being in my family is that

everyone makes an effort to make others happy. My mother cares about my aunts, and they care about her. Even Joe's father, who's not related by birth, is nice to me. When we go away on vacation, he watches my dog.

"I wish I could have always lived with my natural mother and father, but that didn't happen. If I had to have a step-father, I'm glad it's Joe."

DOUGLAS AGE 12½

"A house should be peaceful"

"About five years ago, my parents got divorced. When they decided to break up, I felt miserable most of the time. Suddenly, after doing so well in school, I lost interest in my work, and my grades began to slip. Mostly I dreaded hearing my parents argue with each other. They just couldn't get along, and that's why their marriage fell apart.

"It was also hard not knowing any other children in the same situation. My friends acted as if I was weird. They couldn't understand what was going on in my life, but neither could I. A year and a half later, when Dad told me he was marrying Pat, I was relieved to be back in a family. Although this was Dad's third marriage (his first was when he was in law school), I thought he and Pat could make things work. In my mind, marriage was supposed to last. It was my parents who were strange for divorcing."

Since his parents' separation and divorce, Douglas and his older brother, Daniel, have alternated homes each week. "When their marriage broke up, Mom moved into her own apartment, while Dad kept the house. Because they lived so close to each other, joint custody worked out.

"In my opinion, switching homes every week is rotten. Of all the things that happened because of the divorce, that's been the hardest for me. I'm better adjusted to it than I was, but it's still confusing.

"At Dad's I live with three rowdy brothers—Daniel plus my stepbrothers, Owen and Eric—and our dog, Rudy. There, my bedtime is eleven o'clock. When I go to Mom's, I'm in a totally different atmosphere. Her house is so quiet with just the two of us, since Daniel's usually off with his friends. Bedtime at Mom's is ten o'clock. After having been at Dad's, I'm not tired then, so for the first night or two, I have trouble falling asleep. When I finally get settled in, I have to move again."

To make his life easier, Douglas keeps clothing at both places. But each week he has to bring some extras, depending upon the weather or school activities. "It never fails that I forget one small thing and have to go back to the other house to get it. That can be a real pain, especially for the person who has to drive me.

"Having two different homes can be embarrassing, too. Sometimes in school I'm asked to write on forms that don't have enough lines for my two different addresses. It's annoying having to explain why I need another sheet of paper."

. . . .

Once his father married Pat, Douglas had another adjustment to make: living with two stepbrothers. In the beginning there were many awkward situations. "Although
I feel close to Owen and Eric today, it didn't happen overnight. During those early months, I had no idea what to
talk about with them or how we should play together. Gradually, we worked things out.

"One thing in particular helped us get along better—our
dog, Rudy. From the moment he arrived, we shared responsibilities: feeding and walking him, and cleaning up
his mess. Rudy was the one subject we didn't fight about.
We even played with him together without arguing."

When Douglas and Daniel's father remarried, Owen and
Eric began attending their stepbrothers' school. "Owen and
I were both in fourth grade, but in different classes. On
the first day of school, I introduced him to my friends as
my stepbrother, not knowing how they would react. Fortunately, Owen gets along well with everybody and was
quickly accepted. Since he's also good in sports, it made it
easier for him to join in. Pretty soon I started thinking of
him as my school friend, rather than my stepbrother.

"Now Owen and I are in seventh grade, and we do well.
We both have lots of friends; some we share, and some we
don't. And we're good athletes. The only time we compete
is when we're playing on opposite teams.

"The best thing about having Owen for a stepbrother is
that we're the same age. That means we can help each
other in math or go to parties together. Although we're not
biologically related, Owen's definitely part of my family.

Douglas and Rudy

. . . .

"Having lived with him and Eric for four years, I'm glad they're my stepbrothers. Even though we have different last names I consider them my brothers.

"Still, the stepfamily arrangement is not always easy. For one thing, being the youngest and smallest of the kids, I get all the hand-me-downs. Of course, if I *really* need something, Mom or Dad will get it for me, but first I have to explain why it has to be something new.

"Also, because Owen is seven months older than I, he thinks of himself as my big brother and sometimes acts a little cocky. And because he's older, things happen to him first. Although I started Hebrew school before he moved here, he had his Bar Mitzvah and got all the attention and gifts ahead of me. While I'm looking forward to my celebration, I wish it had come before his."

As for his relationship with Pat, Douglas liked her from the start—even before she married his father. "I'd see Pat when I was staying at Dad's house and she'd come to visit. One weekend, after Pat and Dad had been dating for a while, her family and ours got together and played baseball. While I can't remember anything about the wedding day, I'll never forget that baseball game. It was great.

"Of all the adults in my family now, I have the most fun with Pat. She's home more than the others because she doesn't work, so I get to do a lot of things with her. Since we're the only two who like eating Thai food, we go to those restaurants together. More than that, Pat gives me a lot of attention. Besides being a nice person and a great cook, she's a good listener."

The only time Douglas becomes uncomfortable with his stepmother is when the subject of his parents' divorce comes up. "Pat takes my father's side and sees things from his point of view. But I remember *both* of my parents arguing all the time, so I can't say who's most at fault.

"Anyhow, my mother will always be my parent, and that will never change. I guess that's why I don't like anyone talking badly about her. Sometimes Mom does things that upset me, but other times she's there when I need her. While I realize that she and Dad couldn't make it together, at least I know they both love me.

"When Dad married Pat, I thought I'd finally be in a normal family. In my head, a divorced family was peculiar. Thinking about my life today, I see that I've landed in a more unusual setup than I expected. But fortunately, things have turned out all right.

"Still, I have some questions about my future. After all I've been through, marriage might be a problem for me. I wouldn't want to get divorced and go through the kind of arguing I heard between Mom and Dad. I'll never forget how upset Mom was at that time."

Arguing—especially between his parents—continues to make Douglas anxious. "Once in a while Mom and Dad have a fight on the phone. Usually they disagree about small things. Even so, I don't like to hear them raise their voices. It reminds me of what went on during the divorce years. Thank goodness they're much better than they used to be, and I can count on them getting along in public.

"Pat and Dad have fights, too, but just little ones. Still,

. . . .

that makes me nervous. I think, What if *they* don't make it?"

In Douglas's fantasies, the ideal family would include a dog like Rudy, a cute baby girl like his new cousin, two nice brothers who have the same ability in sports and can have fun together, and, to make life easier, the original parents. "Most important, everyone has to get along. I realize families have to have an occasional fight, but a house should be peaceful.

"As for being in a stepfamily, I've pretty much gone with the flow. Now I can't imagine what I'd be like if Pat, Owen, and Eric hadn't come into my life. Surely I'd be a different person than I am today, and I'm happy to be me. That alone makes me believe that everything will work out in my future."

OWEN AGE 13

"There's no way to predict how things will work out"

Owen's father died when he was six months old. "I have a lot of pain when I think about my dad. And for a long time I was angry that he died. Mom took me to a therapist when I was in second grade, and after going for three years, I felt much better."

While Owen was in therapy, his mother started dating Ron. "Mom had gone out with lots of guys, but she liked Ron the best. Still, I had no idea how serious she was with him or what the man was really like. The few times I spoke to him were when he came to our apartment to pick Mom up. He seemed nice.

"Then one day Mom told me that Ron had invited the three of us to his house. I suspected something was up because my older brother, Eric, agreed to come along. That Sunday visit made an impression on me. Even though Eric and I had never met Daniel and Douglas—Ron's two boys—before, we all had a lot of fun playing baseball."

After that weekend the two families went on ski trips together, visited museums, and even shared holidays. When Owen's mother had known Ron for a year, she told Owen and Eric that she would be getting married the following September. "Mom also announced that, three weeks before the wedding, we would be moving into a new house in the suburbs. That way Eric and I could begin the school year with everyone else. Although Eric was upset about leaving the city, it didn't bother me. In a way, I was ready for the change. In fact, I had no objections to anything she told us. Having never been in a stepfamily, I couldn't imagine what it would be like—good or bad—and decided to wait and see.

"But moving before the wedding scared me to death. What if Mom suddenly decided not to go through with the marriage, after giving up our apartment and her job, and switching our schools? Thank goodness everything turned out well, but those were three long weeks.

"After that, my life really changed. Until Mom's marriage, there were just three people in my house. Within minutes, our family doubled in size."

Before Owen's mother married Ron, the two families met a few times so everybody could talk about their concerns. While Owen doesn't remember what was discussed at these meetings, he says they at least helped him feel more comfortable with his future stepfather. "There's no way to predict how things will work out. You have to live with people to understand what they're about. For me, the biggest issue became getting used to a second adult in the house. For almost my entire life, I only had to listen to my mother. Now suddenly Ron was in charge, too, and he did things differently from the way I had been brought up.

"From the start, Ron was stricter than Mom. While he wasn't real harsh, he grounded me or sent me to my room when I misbehaved. Even today, he punishes me that way.

"Mom, on the other hand, was always lenient with Eric and me. As soon as she remarried, though, *she* started disciplining us more, too. It took me a while to get used to this, and I'm still not thrilled with how she's changed.

"What makes it harder is that my stepfather relaxes the rule when it comes to disciplining Douglas. I admit that Douglas doesn't talk back to his father as much as I do, but it's still not fair."

Despite these feelings, Owen has no fantasies about living with his biological father instead. "Maybe if I had known my dad better, I would feel differently. But there's no sense wishing for the kind of person who may never have existed. I was so young when Dad died that I have no memories of him. Whatever I create in my mind about him is just make-believe.

"At least with all the people in my family today, I don't get bored around here. But at times it's hard living with so many different personalities. I never realized how much energy it takes learning how to behave with each individual. It can be years before some things are worked out. Truthfully, if I had to do it over, I would have been less cautious with my stepbrothers. It's easy to say that now, because I trust them and like them a lot. When I first met them, though, I kept my distance."

Owen's acceptance of his stepbrothers was complicated by the fact that he and Douglas were in the same grade (as were Eric and Daniel). And Owen's stepbrothers live alternate weeks with their mother. "Even though it's hectic with the four of us together, in some ways it's easier for me. The weeks Douglas and Daniel are away, Eric and I fight. But when Eric has Daniel to hang out with, my brother and I get along pretty well.

"I've discovered other advantages to having a big family, too. For one, there's a variety of people around, and always someone to do something with. If I want to shoot baskets, I ask Eric or Daniel, who are stronger and more challenging. If I want to walk around the village, I choose Douglas, since we're in the same grade and have a lot in common. When I need to talk to somebody, I go to Daniel, who's interested in what I have to say. I have fun with my brother, Eric, too, but unfortunately he insists on treating me like a kid."

Owen noticed a big change in his feelings about his family after they spent a summer vacation together. "Two years ago, the six of us went to the beach. With everyone away from the house, school, and work, we were all much calmer. By the end of the holiday I started thinking about Douglas and Daniel as my real family.

"Other changes—some big, some little—helped me enjoy being with the family more, too. For one, I disliked family

Owen, left, and Douglas with Rudy

meals because they were so noisy. Then, a few months ago, Mom started serving in the dining room. Somehow the formal setting quieted everyone down. Although we haven't turned into saints, we have fewer arguments than before. Now when Mom calls us to eat, I think of the event as a special occasion.

"Getting a dog—Mom's idea—helped cement the combined families. When Rudy came to our house, everyone was immediately attached to him. Even Eric, who's not the most gentle, laid-back person, acted mellow around Rudy. While we're a family that can argue over silly things, we all agree about what's good for our dog. Nobody complains when it's his turn to take Rudy out.

"Another thing that helped my family become closer was my interest in Judaism, and my Bar Mitzvah. I owe that to Ron and his sister's strong religious feelings. Mom was never all that religious and she hadn't bothered to enroll Eric or me in Hebrew school. But Ron took Douglas and Daniel to Sunday school. I watched them go each week and, having nothing to do, asked Mom if I could join, too. From the start I enjoyed the whole experience. While a lot of the kids in the class griped that Hebrew school was a drag, I didn't mind it at all. In fact, I'm still going, even though I already had my Bar Mitzvah."

At Owen's Bar Mitzvah, all of Ron's relatives and Owen's, too, were together in one place for the first time. "It meant so much to me that I decided to make that the subject of my speech. And now that I know a lot about the holidays, celebrating them is more special. Sometimes Ron's parents,

Grandpa Lou and Grandma Belle, come up from Florida, which is even better.

"Because all of us have worked so hard, my stepfamily situation has improved. Years back, I never would have dreamed that I could feel the way I do about everyone I live with today. Now that I'm getting older I understand that, although my stepfamily and I are not related by birth, it's still possible to feel very close to each person."

TRACY AGE 27

"The last thing I wanted was change"

"Though I was only three when I became a stepchild, I was affected by all the changes that came with remarriage. When Mom first told me that Jim would be her husband, I fantasized that everything would now be normal and wonderful for me. Like other kids, I'd have a mommy and a daddy, and we'd live in our own house. From the way Mom was talking, I'd even have lots of brothers and sisters, which was what I wanted.

"But things didn't turn out to be so simple. For one, it hurt when we moved an hour away from my grandparents and uncle. Mom and I had lived with them for the year following my parents' divorce. Although I still felt close to them after the move, our relationship was never the same again. Even more unsettling was getting used to my stepfather's huge family, with whom I had nothing in common.

29

I might have been little then, but I remember feeling insecure."

Tracy's stepfather, whom she called Dad, tried hard to assure her of his love. "From the start, Dad treated me like his own daughter. He had never been married before, and for three years—until my brother was born—I was his only child. He said more than once that he fell in love with me the moment we met, which made it easier for him to marry Mom.

"The year before my brother was born, Dad adopted me. In retrospect, it was the best thing he could have done. Since in all ways he fit the bill as my dad, giving me his last name was lasting proof that he wanted me for his child."

Soon after, Tracy had to adjust to a baby in the family and a second move, this one even farther away from her relatives. Moving also meant that Tracy started first grade in a new school. "Every morning as I left the house, I felt jealous seeing Mom with the baby. As soon as my brother, Greg, was born, I was sure he had replaced me as the special child. I thought, Now that Mom and Dad have their own son, I'll be off to the side, while he gets the most attention. In reality I was always Daddy's little girl, but inside I didn't believe it, and I took my anger out on my brother.

"Whenever Greg wanted to play with me, I pushed him away or said something mean. For some reason, when Greg was around, I never felt I completely fit in. Finally, when he was older and out of the house more, I relaxed.

. . . .

"A little while ago I decided to talk to a counselor, who has helped me understand my feelings. Only recently have I been able to ask my brother's forgiveness. I told him that I treated him so poorly because of my negative feelings about myself."

About six months before her brother was born, Tracy saw her biological father for the first time since her parents had separated. Until then, she hadn't even talked to him. Although Tracy knows that she and her father did finally meet, she has no memory of that visit. "I probably blocked him out of my mind because I was so angry that he had disappeared from my life. Anyhow, by then I felt completely accepted by my stepfather, and I didn't want another dad to complicate things. It had taken me a while to feel comfortable in my new family. The last thing I wanted was change.

"But when I became a teenager, I started thinking about him. I guess I was curious about which characteristics of his I had inherited. Mostly I wanted to know why he had given me up for adoption. At that time, too, I was in a rebellious stage. After having been so content with Dad— my stepfather—I started calling him James. Although he was the last person I'd confide in then, now I wish I had told him how alone I felt. I think he would have been sympathetic. My grandmother, trying to help, gave me an old photograph of my father and told me what he was like. But that wasn't enough. I wanted to talk to him in person.

"With all my searching, I never got together with my biological father. Only recently have I found out where he's living. But now that I can call him, I'm afraid to make the first move. Probably he feels the same."

Looking back, Tracy sees a lot of positive things that her stepfather brought to her life. "I loved Dad a lot. As I got older I could see elements of his personality in me, especially his sense of humor. Also, Dad taught me that every story has two sides. When I used to describe arguments I had with other people, he'd explain my part in the fight, too. Dad was a great listener and full of good advice.

"With time I learned to get along with Dad's large family. Through the years we saw a lot of his relatives, and I grew very close to them. None of them ever made me feel I wasn't accepted. In fact, six years ago, when my son was born, Mommom—my stepgrandmother—marveled at how the baby resembled her side of the family. She'd forgotten we weren't really related."

Although Tracy's family didn't have much money (her stepfather was a seasonal truck driver), they still managed to have fun. "Dad's imagination and spontaneity helped get us through. For instance, in the summer we drove cross-country to visit relatives in California. Dad, being an adventurer, would make a wrong turn and continue on that road. Once we landed at a ghost town, which I loved.

"Still, if it had been possible, I would have grown up with my two original parents, just as my brother and all my friends did. It was so hard not knowing other kids whose parents had divorced and remarried. Besides thinking my family was odd, I felt alone. I never told anyone that Dad wasn't my real father.

"It's too bad that schools at that time didn't have counselors to help children sort out their feelings. Maybe then I wouldn't have lived so long with my insecurity about not belonging. Though I talked to Mom and Dad about many subjects, that one I kept to myself."

Yet Tracy gives her mother credit for being honest whenever she asked her questions. "Mom was very frank and told me as much as I could handle at the time. If I ever had a problem, I knew I could go to her. For some reason, though, I still kept my most painful thoughts inside me. For example, each time Mom and Dad argued, I worried. Although they didn't fight that much, if I heard them yelling I thought, Oh no, this marriage will end too. Of all things, I dreaded that most. The worst fight was when one of them drove away afterward. For the moment, I thought everything was over. Thank goodness they're still together, living a few minutes away from me."

Now Tracy is married and has two children of her own, a boy and a girl. "My parents' divorce made me grow up quickly. I took on emotional things that I wasn't ready to handle. Other children of divorce whom I've spoken to say they feel the same way. While I still deeply love my stepfather, I hope my children grow up with their original parents—that is, if the parents love each other. But people make mistakes and, knowing myself, I wouldn't want to stay in a bad marriage. So divorce sometimes has to be.

"I often think about how fortunate I've been to have my stepfather, and how, from day one, he made me feel I was part of his family. I'm thankful that he passed down so much good to me which I, in turn, can pass on to my kids."

BRIAN AGE 23

"All I could think was,
How could Dad let another woman
take Mom's place?"

Before his father remarried, Brian and his family celebrated Christmas Eve at his future stepmother's house. "Marge gave everybody outstanding gifts. When I opened mine, my mouth dropped in amazement. It was a television game, the most expensive present anyone had ever bought me. Here Marge wasn't even my mother yet, but she was treating me special. I wasn't sure if this was a way to buy me off or if she was being just plain nice. To keep on the safe side, I maintained a cautious distance. Nevertheless, I'll always remember how wonderful that gift made me feel.

"I was twelve when my father married Marge, a widow who had inherited a lucrative business. Five years before that, my mother died after a long illness. Except for the first six months after my mother's death, when my grandma stayed with us, Dad was a single parent for my three older brothers, my older sister, and me until he remarried. Unfortunately, he wasn't reliable then, emotionally or financially—because he drank. To survive, we five kids stuck close together and helped each other out.

"As the youngest, I always had someone to take care of me. I could always count on Richie or Carl, my two oldest brothers, to make sure I was safe. For example, when I was younger and visited friends, they'd come to get me before it got dark. But still, it wasn't like having a mom.

"You'd think then that I'd have been happy when Dad announced one Sunday, on the way to church, that he was marrying Marge. Besides being well off, Marge was an okay person. Although I liked her and her two college-aged kids, Paul and Iris, whom I had known for a year, I didn't want Marge in the family. All I could think was, How could Dad let another woman take Mom's place?"

Brian confided in his brothers and sister, hoping to get their sympathy. "Since Richie was already in college and Carl was getting ready to leave, Marge's coming into the family didn't seem like a big deal to them. Even my sister, Susan, and brother Danny, who were still at home, didn't seem to mind. They thought it was a good idea for Dad to have a companion and tried to assure me that things would work out.

"But Marge was a sixth grade teacher, and this really worried me because I didn't do so great in school. I knew Marge wouldn't stand for that! During the years Dad was alone, I was a free child. Instead of doing my homework, I spent the time playing football and baseball. Basically I was a good kid, but from time to time I got in trouble. Now and then Dad grounded me, but mostly I got by without punishment because my father was too out of it, from drinking, to stay on top of things."

Soon after the marriage, Brian convinced himself further that his stepmother, whom he now called Mom, and he would never make it together. "She was a believer in rules, hard work, and good behavior, while I was a mischievous, fun-loving kid."

When Marge tried to set up household routines, Brian rebelled. "I kept thinking, My real mother would never have been as demanding. No way would she have insisted that I do three hours of chores every Saturday, while my friends were out biking. She never would have made me pull the weeds from the patio or take the laundry off the line. Each time I had to do a job for my stepmom, I'd start off cooperatively but end by messing up.

"More and more I missed the old days, when it was just Dad. Then, no one told us kids what to do. We just cleaned up the house when it needed it. Even mealtimes were easier. If I was hungry, I just grabbed something, usually frozen waffles from the fridge." Marge, though, expected the adults and children to sit down as a family for a nutritious dinner each night. "She made sure vegetables were on the menu every evening."

Brian's resentment of his stepmother increased when his dad backed her up. "Our different ideas about what a twelve-year-old could do caused bigger problems as soon as she got my father on her side. Suddenly, he too insisted that I study more and apply myself. During the week, I was no longer allowed to leave the house at night, and every evening, Mom checked my homework. It was bad enough having my stepmother on my case, but it hurt that Dad was being pulled away from me. More and more I was convinced that my family had been fine without Mom on the scene.

"At least I had an ally in Susan. She also resented Mom for telling her what to do. Every morning we poured out our feelings to each other in the bathroom as Susan fixed her hair. Just listening to my sister's complaints added fuel to my fire."

The angrier Brian became with his stepmother, the more he thought about his biological mom. "Although I hardly remembered her, I could recall some pleasant things we did together. For instance, she took me everywhere with her in the car, and sometimes she'd take me out for lunch as a treat. If I ordered a hot dog, she'd ask the waitress to cut it into little pieces, since she knew I didn't like it on a roll. With my real mother, I never felt odd.

"But with a stepmother, I stood out. All my friends lived with their original parents. Having a stepmother made me feel different. No teenager wants to be different, and I was no exception. More than once I broke down, wishing my real mother was alive.

"Then when I was thirteen, Mom told Dad that he had to quit drinking or she would leave. When Dad came home drunk one night, Mom packed up and left for a few days to give him time to think things over. On the one hand, I was happy to see her go. On the other, I thought, If she loved us she wouldn't do this. Deep down I felt hurt. The outcome of that night was that Dad never took another sip of alcohol. That was ten years ago."

Looking back on his growing-up years, Brian regrets much of his behavior with Marge. He attributes it to adolescence and the upheaval he lived with while his father was a single parent. "I definitely was a rotten kid for giving Mom such a hard time. Worse, though, I hurt myself in the end. Too bad I was almost a teenager when Dad married Mom. At that age, in particular, I didn't want anyone bossing me around, especially a stranger. Probably I—and my sister Susan, too—would have acted the same with my real mother, who, my brothers have confided recently, wasn't all that perfect.

"Only now, being more mature and having had counseling, do I understand that Mom wanted me to achieve for my own sake. She tried to steer me in the right direction, but I kept fighting her. If I had followed her advice back then, I would have saved myself a lot of hassles. Instead, I thought I knew everything."

Most of all, Brian credits Marge for helping his father get on the right track. He stopped drinking and became a dependable parent and husband. "As soon as they married, Dad took over Mom's first husband's business, and our family's finances immediately improved. We went on vacations to Disney World, and I got new sneakers and clothes when I needed them.

"To be honest, I have good memories of about 50 percent of the time I lived with Mom. Although I wouldn't have admitted it back then, she actually added fun to my life. For one thing, she had a large family that we saw often. I hardly knew most of my own relatives, who lived far away. On holidays like Memorial Day and the Fourth of July, Mom invited her troops, which I loved. With all the stepaunts, -uncles, and -cousins, I felt I was part of a real family.

"Although I never got to know my stepsister, Iris, well because she was away at college year round, I was very close to my stepbrother, Paul. Every holiday and vacation when he came home, we waxed his car or played baseball together. Whenever I was with Paul, I felt good.

"I owe it to Mom, too, that I was even more comfortable with my friends. After Dad remarried, I was happy to invite the guys to my house, which I wouldn't have done years back. And when Mom and Dad put in a pool—among the first in the neighborhood—*my* backyard became the hangout."

Today Brian says that, compared to what went on in the past, his relationship with his stepmother is great. He sees her now and then on weekends. "While Mom still bugs me at times, I'm able to see now how hard she worked to keep my family together. For that alone, I'm thankful. Mainly because *I've* changed, my relationship with Mom has changed. I went through a lot growing up, and when people tried to push me in a certain direction, it didn't work until I was ready. Luckily, I started to improve my grades during the last year and a half of high school. I even got A's in some of my classes. I went to college for one year but didn't finish."

Brian's sister, Susan, also mellowed in her relationship

with their stepmother. "After Susan graduated from high school, she went to secretarial school for one year. When she came home at night, Mom helped her with her studies. Gradually, she and Mom started getting along better, although they still have their disagreements."

Now twenty-three, Brian is married and has a three-month-old daughter. "To me, family is so important. All through my life I always knew that if I needed my brothers and sister, they would be there to give me a hand.

"Today my dream is to buy a house for my own family—not a mansion, but a little one with a white picket fence around it. Right now I'm working two jobs so I can save some money to make sure this dream comes true.

"More than anything, I hope the family my wife and I raise will be a close and happy one. I have a lot of love to give, and I believe that if there's love in a house, things work out."

MARY AGE 11 ½

"I was sure my stepfamily would never work out"

"In my original family, there were six kids. As the youngest, I got the most attention. And there was always someone to take care of me. When my mother was sick, my sister Laurie, who's now seventeen, tucked me into bed at night and talked to me. After Mom passed away, I went to Dad for comforting. At first, I wasn't used to telling him my problems—I had always confided in Mom—but as soon as he saw my sad face, he'd hug me and I'd feel better.

"My mother had cancer for three years before she died. I was nine at the time. A year later, my father married Darlene, whom I now call Mom. With her two children, Harry James and Annette, my family grew to ten. Luckily, two of my older sisters and one brother are away at school most of the time, which makes our house a little quieter. Still, my brother Nick's at home, as is my oldest sister,

. . . .

Kristen, who has cerebral palsy. She's in a wheelchair and needs special care."

Mary only recently learned how long her mother was seriously ill. "For the first year or two my mother looked okay to me, so I didn't think she was so sick. In fact, I thought she had asthma, because she used a breathing device to help her cough less. Besides, she was still well enough for us to go places together—like to my oldest brother's hockey games or to the store. Then she started going to the hospital every Wednesday for treatments, and she'd come home feeling awful. Even so, the next day she'd be up again doing normal stuff. The last year, though, she was very weak and just stayed in bed or on the couch. That's when Dad told me she had cancer. I knew that was a bad disease, but not until the very end did I think she would die.

"Before she got sick, my mother modeled, and sometimes I went with her. Once we entered a mother-daughter modeling contest and won. I still have the picture of us together on my wall. Of all the people in my family, I was closest to my mom. Even thinking and talking about her today makes me feel sad. Especially at night, when I'm lying in bed, I miss her so much that I cry myself to sleep."

The first time Mary met Darlene was on a weekend vacation in Vermont. Before that they had just talked on the phone when Darlene called Mary's father. "Dad had told me that they were good friends, and that she was very nice. I thought so, too, when I met her, and I liked her sister, who came along as well. One night we all went out for dinner: Dad, me, Darlene, her sister, my brother Nick, and my sisters Laurie and Nicole. We had a good time.

"A while after that, everyone got together again. This time my whole family met Darlene and her two kids. I remember that we went to see Santa Claus. By then I knew something was up between Dad and Darlene, but I wasn't sure what. So I said to Dad, fishing, 'It's great that you guys are such good friends.' When he heard this he looked at me, puzzled, and said, 'Mary, we're a lot closer than friends.' I didn't know what that meant. Looking back, I think I didn't want to know."

Finally, a few months before his engagement to Darlene, Mary's father told Mary he was planning to remarry. "Dad explained how hard it was being mother and father to all of us, especially with all the care my sister Kristen needed. Although on weekdays we had someone to come to the house to dress, feed, and stay with her, on weekends Kristen was our responsibility.

"Still, I couldn't understand why Dad wanted a wife when he had six children to keep him company. Besides, I didn't want Dad to be with another woman, and I didn't want to live with a stepmother. After watching so many movies about mean stepmothers and unhappy kids, I was sure my stepfamily would never work out. It was all very confusing."

During this time, Mary confided in her sister Laurie, who also tried to convince her that the family needed a mother. Darlene, Laurie said, seemed like the right person for that role.

"Now that I'm a little older, I think maybe Dad was lonely when he decided to marry. But back then, I was only concerned about myself, not about him. Mostly I wondered how his marriage was going to help any of us, particularly me."

Then Mary's father had more news: The family would be moving to another state so that all of them could start a new life near both sets of grandparents (her father's parents and Darlene's). Darlene, a podiatrist, and Mary's father, a pediatrician, were willing to relocate their practices. "I couldn't imagine anything worse that could happen to me. I wondered how Dad could take me away from the town I was born in and had been part of for nine years. With my mother gone, I needed to keep my life steady, and now Dad was shaking things up. Whenever Dad brought up the subject of moving, I got so upset and angry that I cried.

"Although he tried to assure me that everything would work out okay, I didn't believe him. Only when we finally picked the house, and I met some kids in the neighborhood, did I relax.

"The summer before the wedding, Nick and I went to live with our grandparents while Dad and the older kids packed. Every weekend, Dad and Darlene visited us, and we all went over to the house to see how things were coming along. Pretty soon I made a friend nearby, which helped me. In October, Dad and Darlene were married, and on that same day we moved in together.

"Here I had just had a great time walking down the aisle

and dancing at the wedding, but the minute I walked through the door of our house, I got angry again. All over the place were cartons packed with everybody's stuff. It made me realize more than ever that now I had to live with strangers who were suddenly my family.

"Right away, there were changes in my life. With Harry James, six, and Annette, five, I was no longer the baby of the family. In the beginning, that was the hardest thing for me to accept. I was jealous every time Dad played with my stepbrother and stepsister. Whenever he asked me to do him a favor I made a face, which I'd never done before."

Mary's expectations of the "mean" stepmother didn't help that relationship, either. "Mom would come home from work with a toy for her own kids but nothing for my brother Nick and me. Both Nick and I thought she purposely forgot us. Instead of telling her how hurt we were, we snubbed her. This went on for a while, until she figured out the problem and started bringing home gifts for us, too. It didn't matter how small they were. We just wanted to be remembered. Especially when stepfamilies are new, it's the little things parents do that count the most.

"The longer I've been in a stepfamily, the more I see that movies don't show things the way they really are. My stepmother isn't mean at all. If anything, she's on my side. From the minute she married Dad, she didn't try to take my mother's place, but acted more like a friend—helping me with my homework and being affectionate when I needed it. Even today, she says the right things when I come to her with my problems. She tells me that the stuff that bothers me now upset her when she was my age. Hearing that makes me realize I'm not the only one in the world with troubles.

"Sometimes when we go to Grandma's house, Mom shows me pictures of herself as a little girl and describes what her life was like then. That's been a good way for me to get to know her better, too.

"Because of my stepmother, I've learned that family doesn't only mean having the same last name and blood. What's most important is that we can trust and depend on one another."

With each day, Mary feels closer to her stepmother and sees that their relationship keeps changing. "Today my stepmother's like a friend and a mother, combined. Sometimes it's hard for me to tell the difference. Not that I've forgotten my first mother. I think about her a lot. It makes me sad, remembering the times we were together."

Ever since her mother's death, Mary has felt even closer to her father. "Years ago the only time Dad and I would be alone was when he read me bedtime stories. Today, we go off together without the other kids. It may be just a trip to the supermarket, or sometimes Dad takes me to the hospital when he goes on rounds. Then we have the whole morning to ourselves and I get to watch him take care of the newborn babies. They're so cute.

"Now I feel much more comfortable telling Dad my problems. What's good about Dad is that he doesn't even have to say a word when I feel bad. Just a hug and a kiss from him let me know things will be okay.

"Luckily, I have a lot of people in my family to comfort me if I need it. Even Nick, whom I fight with, is a great brother. We talk to each other when we're mad at Mom or Dad and help each other out.

"Also, there're my grandparents—Dad's mother and father—who live in the next town. Talking to Nanny and Poppy before Dad got married was just what I needed." Darlene's parents, too, live close by.

"Being in a stepfamily hasn't been easy for me. But I see that problems can be worked out if I talk about them. At least now I'm no longer afraid to tell Mom or Dad how I feel.

"Although I've never spoken to a counselor or been in a school group with other kids in stepfamilies, I sometimes confide in my friend Keri, who also has a stepparent. Her parents are divorced, so her situation is a little different. Lately I've noticed that I've been listening more to Keri's problems than talking about my own, but even she isn't complaining so much.

"In a way, I consider myself lucky. For the first nine years of my life, I had a great mom. And now I have another great mom. If I had to make a choice between the two of them, I couldn't pick one over the other.

"I see that if a stepmother or -father takes care of you and puts in the time to make things better, then they're Mom or Dad all the way."

Looking back over the past few years, Mary thinks she's grown up a lot. "I act better than I did when Dad first remarried. Now I don't compete for attention with Annette and Harry James but behave more like a big sister to them. I don't even mind being their babysitter once in a while. Though it took some time for me to like them, I've finally started thinking of the three of us as good friends." In fact, as she and the two younger children have gotten closer, Mary worries that she's drifting away from her biological siblings who are away at school. "More than anything, I don't want that to happen. I love my family and want us to always be there for each other.

"It's hard to believe that I'm only eleven and a half and have been through so much. I was really sad for a long time, starting when my mother got sick. Recently that's changed. In the past, there were moments when I wanted to give up, but I'm glad I didn't. With Dad and Mom at my side, I've learned to have hope."

KERI AGE 11

"I didn't want a stepfather—
any stepfather"

"My friend Mary and I started at a new school at around the same time. Since we didn't know many kids, we hung out together. Mary told me she moved to the neighborhood because her mom had died and her father had just re-married. When I said that my mom had just remarried, too, we had a lot to talk about."

Keri still remembers the day her parents separated. "I was six then and had just come home from my friend Candace's house. Mom took me aside and explained that Dad was moving out. As soon as I saw Dad getting ready to go, I ran up to my room, shut the door, and cried. Even though my parents fought so much, I still didn't want their marriage to end."

For the next three years, Keri's father lived with his mother, Keri's grandma, while Keri and her mom stayed in their old house. "In the beginning, it felt weird when

Dad didn't come home at night. Worse, it seemed like he hardly visited me. I thought that if Mom hadn't asked for the divorce, this wouldn't be happening. Especially then, I was angry at her for messing up my life, and I was mad at Dad for not coming to see me enough.

"Even when I did spend the weekend with Dad, it wasn't much fun. He used to say bad things about Mom and tell me that he was against getting divorced. Finally Mom took me to a therapist a few times, where I learned how to express my feelings to Dad. After that, I started enjoying the visits more.

"Some days Dad and I went to the movies or bowling. Other times we just hung out at Grandma's. If it was warm enough, we fed the birds and ducks at a nearby lake, which we still do today."

Even while she missed her father, Keri admits she liked having her mother to herself. "As soon as Mom got home from work, we'd eat dinner together and then talk or watch TV. It was great, just the two of us. But Mom started dating Tom when I was seven, and when he came over, everything changed."

Tom, a lawyer, was also divorced. He had two daughters, Erin and Megan, who were older than Keri. "In the beginning, Mom saw Tom when I was on weekend visits with Dad. But pretty soon she invited him to dinner. He was pretty nice—always in a good mood, joking around. Soon I realized, though, that Mom was serious about him. That made me mad, because I knew Mom would now have less time for me.

"From then on, I made up my mind that I didn't like

Keri and her mother

Tom. If he talked about boring subjects at the dinner table,
I made a face. When he asked me questions, I'd give one
word answers or ignore him completely. As soon as he was
gone, Mom would say to me, 'You know, you could have
been more polite to Tom,' and I'd reply, 'Why should I be?
He's not my father.' "

After they'd known each other for a year and a half, Keri's
mom and Tom made plans to marry. "Mom announced
their plans while we were at Tom's house. Erin and Megan
were there, too, and my cousin Stephanie. When I heard
the news, I started crying in front of everyone. 'No! No!' I
kept saying.

"I didn't want Mom to marry, and I didn't want it to be
Tom—especially because I knew we'd have to move into
his new home. For me, that meant going to another school
and leaving my friends."

Now Keri tried harder than ever to get her parents back
together again. "Whenever Dad called to talk to me, I'd tell
him Mom wanted to speak to him, too, and quickly put her
on the phone. My plan never worked. Almost as soon as
they started speaking to each other, the conversation ended
in a fight. Finally, I gave up trying.

"But then I became angrier at Mom. I kept thinking, If
she hadn't wanted a divorce, I wouldn't be going through
this. Every day I told her I didn't like Tom, and every day
she'd try to convince me that he was a nice man. When I
said I felt miserable about leaving my friends, Mom said
that I'd make new ones and things would be okay. But I
didn't believe her.

"At the wedding, when the priest said to Tom, 'You may now kiss the bride,' I'm the only one in the pictures with a sour face."

When Keri and her mom moved into Tom's place, Keri distanced herself even more from the adults. "If Mom came home from work and talked to Tom first, I sulked. If I saw them sitting together on the couch, I walked around the house with a frown, refusing to tell Mom what was bothering me. How could I tell her I didn't want a stepfather—*any* stepfather.

"Mom tried ways to set up situations where Tom and I would be alone together, like suggesting we buy some stuff at the bakery. Immediately, I'd say, 'I'm not going,' but when Tom would start to leave without me, I'd change my mind. Those trips weren't great, but they weren't awful, either."

At least Keri had her stepsisters to look forward to. Although they lived with their mother, they visited their dad a lot. "Megan stayed over about once a month. And Erin spent her college vacations with us.

"From the beginning, I liked both of them. A few weeks before our parents' wedding, the three of us flew to Florida to vacation with their grandparents. While I felt strange being with people I hardly knew, I still had fun with the girls.

"I get along best with Megan, maybe because she's younger. When she comes over, we go ice-skating, to the movies, or to McDonald's. At night, if the parents go out, we stay home and kid around."

Keri with her stepsisters,
Erin, top, and Megan

During vacations, when Erin lives with Keri's family, she and Keri share the same room. "You'd think that Erin would choose to sleep alone, since there's an empty bedroom with Megan not always here. But my room has the stereo, so that's why she crowds in with me. In the end, it's not so bad. We've learned to work things out. The last time she came home, we made a deal: She promised to keep her belongings on one side of the room if I kept mine on the other. The only time we run into big problems is when our parents get involved in our arguments."

Arguing and fighting are sore points with Keri. She can still remember the quarrels that went on between her mother and father. "Mostly Mom and Dad fought after I had gone to bed, thinking I was asleep. But I heard the yelling and hated it. Even today, I can't stand when people raise their voices, especially when it's Tom arguing with Mom.

"He doesn't do it that often, but when he does I try to get him to stop. It bothers me when he or anyone else yells at my mother. Mom tells me it's natural for people to have disagreements. She says it's more important that they make up and forgive. Still, I don't like it when parents raise their voices."

For a long time after the remarriage, Keri avoided Tom. "But no matter how awful I acted toward him, he never said anything nasty to me or got mean. Mostly he tried to be a friend. One time I needed to make a pillow for Home Economics, and Tom, knowing I'm not great in art, drew the cat I wanted on it. If I got stuck on a homework problem, he helped me, too. Sometimes, though, he made me angry. Once when I asked him to correct my spelling for a book report, he wrote comments up and down the side of my paper. Then I told him he was acting like a teacher.

"I know Tom wants me to do better in school and thinks he can get me to improve. He acts the same with Megan. If *I'm* satisfied with how I'm doing, that's all that's important. I wish Tom could understand that."

Despite her two-year resistance to Tom, Keri has recently begun to mellow. "I've been thinking, If I have to live with Tom, I might as well make the best of things. Besides, he isn't all that bad. He'll drive my friends and me to the movies and not even complain about it. The other day, he surprised me with a tape by my favorite group. I guess he heard me talk about them at the dinner table.

"The best thing about my stepfather is that he sticks up for me when Mom can't see my point. Last Halloween, I got to stay out an hour later because of him. Luckily, Mom doesn't mind if Tom takes my side on small stuff, because she knows he won't interfere if big things about me come up. Then, she and Dad make the decisions. Now that my parents are apart, they agree on most things, especially when it comes to my safety. I'm glad they get along that way.

"Although I wish my parents hadn't divorced, I remember how they argued, and I know that if they had stayed together there would be more problems for me today."

Since her mother's remarriage, Keri's relationship with her father has also changed (although one thing had nothing to do with the other). "Dad recently moved into his own house, which is nice, but now he has a girlfriend, Laura, who's usually there when I visit. That means I don't get to be alone with him as much. Also, Laura's very young—twenty-five—although she looks and acts older. Sometimes I get embarrassed thinking about Dad being with someone almost the same age as my stepsister Erin.

"Despite all these changes in my life, I'm sure that any-one meeting me today would say I have it good. Truthfully, I like things the way they are now—at least most of the time. Some days I'm an only child who gets spoiled a lot. But other days I have Erin and Megan to tell my secrets to. My stepsisters are the best part of Mom's remarriage.

"Even in school I'm happy, and I wouldn't want to be any other place. Although it was hard adjusting at first, I like my friends, and now I'm popular with the cool group.

"As for having Mom all to myself, that's something that can't be. We still play cards together and watch TV, but now Mom sits in the middle, between Tom and me.

"The most important thing is that I have a family with a mother and a father. It doesn't matter if the father is a stepdad. I'm more interested in everyone being kind to one another, and that's what it's finally like in my house."

DIANE AGE 35

"I'll always remember how awful it was, saying I had no dad"

"Just before my fourth birthday, my father died of a liver disease. He had been sick with it for a long time. Mom told me all this later, since I was too young to remember.

"Mom didn't remarry until I was eight. During those in-between years, my older sister, Debbie, Mom, and I lived with Grandma, who took care of us while Mom worked full-time. Because she was gone all day and went out nights, Mom wasn't home much. But with Debbie and Grandma around, I felt secure. Still, I wanted a father like other kids had."

Diane particularly longed for a dad in first grade, when her school asked fathers to help beautify the grounds. "I'll always remember how awful it was, saying I had no dad. It made me feel so different from all the other kids. Suddenly, I realized how much I missed having a father around."

Years later, Diane remembered these feelings when she considered divorcing her first husband. "I couldn't believe that, of all people, *I* was taking Keri's father away from her. While I hated putting my daughter in that situation, I knew the marriage wasn't good for me.

"To this day, Keri wishes I hadn't broken up with her dad, despite her vivid memories of our fighting. She still blames me for the divorce.

"Although Keri and I were more like friends than mother and daughter during the three years we lived together, I was still lonely. One Christmas the tree suddenly fell down, and as Keri stood there crying, I had to lift it up and re-decorate it. Then, especially, I felt so alone.

"When I married Tom, I realized that Keri didn't want a stepdad, any stepdad. Then she'd have to share me. But I believed that after she'd lived with Tom awhile, she'd get to like him. Yet I knew I couldn't push their relationship. All I could do was let Keri know how much I loved her and make sure we spent time together, even just lying next to her on her bed at night."

Diane attributes a lot of her optimistic feelings about stepfamilies to the relationship she had with her own step-father. From the moment her mother introduced her to Ralph, she thought he was nice. "Mostly I liked the idea that there'd be a man in the house. Somehow that made me feel more protected. And I could tell that he was a special guy.

"Ralph had been divorced before he met Mom. He had left his wife because she was an alcoholic. Since it was

Diane with Keri and Tom

unusual then for fathers to have custody of their children, his two older daughters, Eileen and Kathleen, stayed with their mother. In the end, his kids rarely visited him, although he tried so hard to make that possible.

"When I was growing up, divorce was uncommon, and Ralph was the only divorced person I knew. That part of his life embarrassed me. Besides, it went against my family's religion. Grandma, in particular, did not approve of a divorced man, so when we got together before the marriage, Mom, Debbie, and I would meet Ralph at his apartment."

From the start, Diane considered Ralph her father. "While Mom was getting dressed for the wedding, I wondered aloud if Ralph would mind if I called him Dad. Mom told me to ask him, and he said 'Dad' was fine. As I watched the ceremony later on I thought, *Now I have a father.*

"This doesn't mean I didn't think about my biological dad. Especially at night, when I was alone in bed, I remembered him and I felt very sad. More than once, I dreamed of him being in a crowd where I couldn't reach him, or I imagined him driving by, not hearing me yell for him. A few months ago, I dreamed that I finally met him. When I woke up, I cried."

With her mother's remarriage, Diane felt she had a family again. Even though she moved to another town and missed her best friend (she stayed in the same private school), having a father figure was most important to her. "Dad definitely added warmth to our home. I felt so good with him around that I began thinking of him as my real father, too. At the same time, I never forgot my birth father. In my mind, I worked out a place for each of them.

"On the other hand, my sister, Debbie—who was thirteen when our mother remarried—had different feelings about having a stepfather. Debbie had memories of our biological father, and under no circumstances did she want *any* other dad in the picture. Until she was sixteen, she let Ralph know he wasn't *her* dad. Although Debbie was hostile to Dad, Mom never pushed their relationship. Instead, she let Debbie proceed with Ralph at her own pace. With time and maturity, Debbie finally accepted our stepfather, and after that they got along much better."

Looking back on her childhood, Diane realizes how hard she worked to make her stepfather happy. When he expressed an interest in history, she rushed to the library to dig up information so they could talk about it. "Dad also liked to fish. Of all foods, Mom hated fish the most. So when Dad came home with his catch, I'd clean and cook the fish and then we'd share the meal together. I never minded doing all this for him. He was so terrific.

"If there was anything I could do to please him, I'd do it. My number one concern was that Dad stay with our family. Above all, I didn't want to lose him. Whenever he and Mom had a fight, I got physically sick.

"After Mom had been remarried for some time, the topic of adoption came up. Though my father was dead and I loved Ralph, I vetoed the idea. I was partial to my last name and proud of it. Everyone in town knew me by that name, so changing it would be confusing to them and to me. Besides, Mom had kept the spirit of my first father alive by telling me how nice he had been and that I looked like him. She even showed me his letters to her from before their marriage, where he had talked about their wonderful future together. So, when it came to giving away his name, I felt guilty. Anyhow, I knew that my stepfather wouldn't hold my dad's last name against me, nor would keeping it affect our feelings for one another. Still, it bothered me when kids asked why Dad and I didn't have the same name. In a matter-of-fact way, I told them my first father died. That ended the discussion."

Diane was so partial to Ralph as her stepfather that his financial difficulties hardly concerned her, even when the family had only lawn furniture in their living room. "If I wanted something special, I earned money for it by working after school. After a while, I saved enough to go on ski trips, and even bought myself a stereo. Having a lot of money was not that important to me. I was happy enough to get the family I wanted, with a stepfather who was understanding, nonjudgmental, and spoiled me with affection. Best of all, Ralph accepted me as I was."

For that reason alone, Diane's stepfather was the person she confided in most, even more than her mother. "Beginning in third grade, I started getting bad marks in school. Dad never made a big deal about this. Despite my fluctuating grades, I excelled on standardized tests, took advanced science courses in high school, and enrolled in nursing school. Finally, I became a medical research technician. After working for eight years, I'm now a full-time college student. So far I've earned A's on all my exams. My goal is to become a school psychologist. So, in the end, Dad's not getting on my case worked best for me."

Five years ago, Ralph suddenly died of a heart attack. "I

was devastated, and Mom was, too. She still hasn't gotten over it and continues to wear her wedding ring.

"At the funeral, where I saw Eileen and Kathleen, I realized how his own kids had missed out on a wonderful man. Then it hit me that, although I had lived with Dad for so long, Eileen and Kathleen were his real children. That made me angry. Deep down I wanted to be his biological daughter and, at the same time, to have been my first father's child, too. Weird!"

Looking back on her family, Diane says she's grateful her mother remarried someone as special as Ralph. "It makes me realize that things can work out if adults and children are willing to give each other a chance. In my house today, I'm proud that Tom, Keri, and I have come so far. Thank goodness my second marriage is getting better every day, and Keri's become more trusting of Tom. I'm also proud that I work well with my former husband when it comes to Keri's welfare.

"The more I think about it, the more I see that I was lucky that my stepdad and I got on great right from the start. All stepfamilies should work out the way mine did. That experience gives me hope in my own home."

BRUCE AGE 35

"I'll never forget the day
Eddie called me Son."

One morning when Bruce was nine, he woke up to find that his father had left home. Although for some time his dad had been returning from work later and later, Bruce never suspected his parents' marriage was in trouble. "My father's leaving really threw me. I had hardly heard arguing in my house.

"In all honesty, I wasn't that close to my father as a kid. My older sister, Linda, was more attached to him than I was. Still, it hurt that our dad was gone.

"The day after he left, he called and told Mom and my grandma, who lived with us, that he was seeing a woman named Julia, and that he had moved in with her. I'll never forget how Mom cried.

" 'What did our mother do to deserve this?' I asked Linda. There was no one I could talk to other than my sister. I

67

might have confided in Grandma, but it was her son who left the family."

From then on, Bruce, Linda, and Karen, the youngest child, visited their dad every other weekend. When he married Julia two years later, the visiting pattern didn't change. "Typically, my father picked us up at our house and brought us to his place, where we'd spend the day. Julia had a son, too—Emmy—who was a year older than Linda. I liked Emmy, though I hated that he lived with my father and I didn't.

"Julia was Cuban—my father's Spanish—and she cooked wonderful meals of yellow rice with capers and spare ribs. Besides, she was nice. Whenever my sisters and I visited, we had a good time.

"Some days Dad even took us to places like amusement parks. But the minute he brought us home, the mood changed. As soon as we all walked through the door, Mom started yelling at him, saying he had kept us out too late. This, of course, always led to a big fight. Then my father would leave, and Mom would get depressed. In the end, I began to wonder if the fun I had with my father was worth such a price. Finally, when I was twelve, I decided it was easier to be with my friends on the weekends, or to do things with the Boy Scouts, so I started seeing him less."

Even before his father left, Bruce's family didn't have much money. His mother worked as a cleaning woman for a department store. "Once Dad moved out, money was a lot tighter, because he didn't make regular child care payments.

"Mom went to work before I got home from school, and

she returned around midnight. The most I ever saw her on a weekday was for an hour, and that was if I waited up late. While Mom was away, Grandma or my aunt took care of my sisters and me. I particularly liked when Grandma was in charge, because she spoiled me the most.

"On Friday nights and on holidays, Mom took us kids with her to work. After we emptied the garbage pails, we roamed around the store's toy department, which was great. Mom also got me started on a stamp collection by bringing home the canceled foreign stamps she found in wastebaskets. Today I work for the postal service as an assistant manager of the computer department. It's funny that even now I'm in a place that's involved with stamps. Maybe that interest began back then.

"Despite all the energy Mom put into being both mother and father to me, I longed for a man in our house. That's why I was so excited about Eddie.

"I met Eddie the summer I was eleven, when he drove Mom to Scout Camp to bring me home. Before then, Mom had written me that she was dating him and that he was a very nice man.

"As I shook Eddie's hand for the first time, I carefully looked him over. Although he wasn't as handsome as my father, he made a good impression. Also, Eddie had a new apple red Galaxy Ford, the most beautiful car I had ever laid eyes on. Not only did it mean Mom was being driven places instead of having to travel by bus and train, but every week Eddie let me clean his car and complimented me on the good job I did."

Bruce's mother dated Eddie, a widower with three grown

children, for two years. "Only one thing about this relationship embarrassed me. Each time Eddie would get ready
to go home, he'd kiss Mom right in front of us kids. 'Ma,
come on, eh! How old are you?' Linda or I would say. Now
I laugh about it, when I look at what people do today. Still,
she was my mother!

"Even though I was a kid, I realized that with Eddie,
Mom was happier than I had seen her in years. That's why
I was gung-ho all the way when Eddie and she said they
were getting married. Finally Mom would have the man
she wanted, and I'd have the man I thought I needed.

"I'll never forget the day Eddie called me Son. For so
long I had hoped that someone would call me that, and he
was the one who did it."

As soon as Bruce's mother remarried, the family moved
to a neighborhood that was closer to Eddie's relatives.
"While the new neighborhood was certainly an improvement over my old one, I still wished we hadn't left. I guess
I didn't like change. Worse, I missed Grandma, who no
longer lived with us." Bruce also felt uncomfortable with
Eddie's family.

"At first, when I met everyone, I was sure we'd never
make it together. I had been brought up in the Spanish
tradition—reserved and knowing my place. Now I was
among these strangers who were noisy and outgoing. I felt
like a foreigner crossing over to a different land. It took
about a year for me to relax with them. Sharing their holidays, barbecues, and summer vacations helped.

"From the time Mom remarried, I realized that, although

Eddie and my stepfamily were not my blood relatives, they were *my family* who loved me and cared about me. Today I'm thankful to have had wonderful experiences with them while I was still a child. They made me know I belonged.

"Eddie, whom I called Pop from the day of the wedding, drove a truck during the week. To earn extra money, he repaired roofs and fixed plumbing on weekends. Lots of times he took me with him on the job. I learned so much from him that has helped me in my own house. More important, he treated me like a young man and made me feel special."

Still, it took Bruce a while to get used to living with his stepfather. "I wouldn't say Pop was stern or got mad that much; compared to Mom, he was easier. But when he yelled it was something awful. His voice made the house shake. Usually he got angry when one of us kids hadn't done what we were supposed to do. Luckily I was a good kid—not into smoking, drinking, or drugs—and I didn't back talk. Most of the time we lived peacefully, since Mom and Pop rarely argued.

"After Mom remarried, I saw even less of my father. That doesn't mean I forgot him or didn't love him deeply. It's just that, with Pop, I felt so good."

Bruce's sisters, Linda and Karen, weren't as attached to their stepfather and his extended family as Bruce was. "They stayed loyal to our father. For some reason, Linda in particular wasn't as angry as I was when our father left, or when he didn't send us money.

"Sometimes at the dinner table, Linda would bring up

something in conversation about our father. While I said little, I didn't change the subject, either. I wasn't trying to forget him. Inside, I knew that if I needed him, he'd always be there for me. Looking back, I guess I was still angry at him for having made Mom so unhappy."

There was a period though, when Bruce was so mad at his father that he no longer wanted to have his last name. "When I asked Pop to adopt me, he convinced me to give up the idea. He explained that what mattered most was that he and I felt close to each other.

"Luckily, with time, I've been able to forgive. Today I visit my father, and now and then we talk on the phone. At a wedding, a few years ago, he and Mom met again. By then they were able to talk calmly to each other. The first thing my father did was thank Mom for doing such a fine job raising us kids."

Twelve years ago, when Bruce was twenty-three, his stepfather died. "Of all the people in my family, I was closest to him. Pop was there as I grew up, and he taught me so much. I still have a close relationship with the rest of his family."

Today Bruce is married and has a three-year-old daughter. His wife is expecting another baby in a few months. "At night when I come home from work, my daughter runs to me with open arms, yelling, 'Daddy, Daddy.' These are the greatest moments in my life. I may not have all the money in the world, but I'm content with the wonderful family I have."

BONNIE AGE 41

"Other kids had a mother, and I didn't"

One of Bonnie's earliest memories is a sense of trouble at home. "I can remember my mother not being available much as a parent to my brother, Randy, sister, Laurie, and me. Mostly she'd lie in bed behind a closed door, or she'd be hospitalized for long periods of time. Although I was very young, I knew something was wrong, but I didn't know exactly what. When I got older, Dad told me that Mom had serious emotional problems."

Most of the time when Bonnie heard that her mother was in the hospital, she accepted it as normal. "Although I missed her, I was used to my mother being away a lot. So the last time she left, when I was five, I didn't realize she wasn't coming back. About once a month, Laurie, Randy, and I visited her in the medical facility. Or if she was an out-patient, we'd go to see her at her apartment.

All the while, I thought she might still come home. Then, when I was about nine, Dad told me they were getting divorced. I felt horrible, realizing my mother was not going to be living with us anymore.

"Until I was thirteen, Randy, Laurie, and I saw her regularly. One summer, when I was around ten, she rented a lakeside cabin and we vacationed with her for two weeks. I'll always remember how great I felt swimming alongside my mother and going for rides with her in the countryside.

"But fun visits were more the exception. Whenever we three kids were with our mother, we felt like we were walking on eggs. The slightest thing would set her off."

For six years, Bonnie's father was a single parent. "Dad was the original Mr. Mom. Every weekend he took us someplace special. Dad's job was in aviation, and he had his own DC 3. He even hung hammocks in the plane so we kids could rest on flights. Once he flew us to California and another time to Bermuda. If we were going to miss school, he got our assignments beforehand.

"During this time we had a live-in nanny called Miss B. She was more of a baby-sitter/housekeeper than a substitute mother. Although she took care of us and went with the family on trips, she never got involved with our personal problems or our schoolwork."

While Bonnie's father tried hard to be both mother and father to his children, Bonnie felt, in subtle ways, that a piece was missing in her life. "For as long as Dad was a single parent, I noticed that my friends hardly invited me to their homes to play. The same was true with Randy and

Laurie. Since mothers usually arranged these things, I think they felt uncomfortable phoning Dad. What other kids took for granted—shopping for clothes with their mom or having her at their side when they visited the dentist— I couldn't look forward to. This made me realize how different my life was from everyone else's. Other kids had a mother, and I didn't.

"Then, when I was ten, Dad met Phyllis, a widow with four sons. They immediately liked each other and started going out. When he introduced me to her, I found her warm and loving too. Besides being unusually nice, she was pretty. At my age, looks meant a lot. Also, Phyllis had two gorgeous older sons, Doug and Chuck, which didn't hurt. And her younger boys, Don and Steve, were adorable.

"The longer Dad dated Phyllis, the more time the two families spent together. After a while, I considered Phyllis and her four kids good friends. Then, one spring day, I came home and there was Phyllis sitting on the couch, wearing a diamond engagement ring. While I wished Dad had told me beforehand about his wedding plans, I was ecstatic to hear that they were getting married. Now I'd finally have the mother I wanted so much."

With the news of their impending marriage, Bonnie's father and Phyllis also told their children about the house they'd bought in another town. Not one of the seven children wanted to move. "Why would any of us choose to go to a town in the sticks whose name nobody could pronounce? Worse, the place looked like the pits inside. I hated the house as soon as I saw it. Besides needing massive repairs, its six bedrooms meant I might have to double-up with my younger sister.

"After the June wedding, both families traveled to Canada to a summer vacation spot. As September approached, none of us kids wanted to go home. We were all anxious about starting at a school where we didn't know a soul. And we were unhappy about having to live in a horror house.

"But when we walked through the front door we were surprised. Over the summer the house had been totally renovated, and now it was spectacular, with the original six bedrooms divided into eleven."

Thinking about the move today, Bonnie feels that her father and stepmother made the right decision. "It was wise for the whole family to start out fresh and on the same footing. In no time we all adjusted to school and made new friends.

"As far as living together in a stepfamily, we had to take it one day at a time. While I never believed the Cinderella story about bad stepmoms and stepsiblings, I still had no idea what to expect beforehand. But Phyllis, whom I now called Mom, was so warm and loving—how could I not like her? And she liked me, too. We both filled each other's needs. I had the mother I'd wished for, and she had the two daughters—Laurie and me—she'd wanted for so long.

"From the start, Mom used common sense to make this new family unit work. She never said a bad word about my biological mother, nor did she try to make herself number-one Mom with us. She didn't have to. Her just being there to pick up the pieces in our lives was proof enough that she cared."

However, Randy and Laurie didn't share Bonnie's strong positive feelings towards their stepmother. "It's a shame, but my sister and brother thought that loving Mom meant that they were being disloyal to our natural mother. At times they were so hard on Phyllis, I got furious. Even after a stressful visit with our mother, Randy and Laurie still withheld their affection from Phyllis, although they were relieved to come back to a stable home. I think they felt guilty about getting attached to Phyllis, especially since our mother said bad things about her. Despite this, Phyllis seemed to understand Randy and Laurie's feelings and never held it against them."

Randy also didn't have it easy with his new position in the family. "As the oldest child for so long, Randy now resented that Doug, Phyllis's son, displaced him as the firstborn. Through the years, Randy had it hard at home, and I think part of the reason was his losing his family place."

A few months after the remarriage, Bonnie's father adopted Phyllis's children. When the judge asked if anybody had objections, no one said a word, not even Randy. "From then on, Phyllis's boys called my father Dad, and we all had the same last name. Dad loved Phyllis's sons, and Phyllis loved his kids.

"Although remarriage meant that Mom had more children to pay attention to, I always felt she maintained her love for her own kids and managed to love us kids as well.

Bonnie as a child with her family. Standing,
from left to right, Dad, Phyllis, Bonnie, Randy,
Laurie, Doug. Sitting, from left to right,
Steve, Terry, Chuck, Don.

I'm sure there were moments when my stepbrothers weren't happy to share their mother with three other children. And I admit I felt the same about Dad dividing his attention. I distinctly remember being jealous if Dad took one of my stepbrothers for ice cream and didn't ask me. In the end, though, the pluses so outweighed the minuses that a little jealousy was a small price to pay for the family I got.

"A year after Dad and Phyllis married, she had a baby, a girl they named Terry. All of us kids were thrilled. Terry was like *our* baby. None of us minded taking care of her. She was so cute, it was like playing with a puppy.

"Now, with eight children in the house, there was rarely a peaceful moment. Mealtime was a zoo. Every dinner, my sister knocked over a glass of milk, or someone leaned back on a chair and fell over. Poor Dad tried to maintain order with a merit and demerit system, which didn't work. For the most part, though, we were good kids. The worst thing that ever happened was on Halloween one year, when my stepbrother Steve rode on a horse through town with a sheet over his head. It ended up with a call from the police."

In retrospect, Bonnie describes the years in her stepfamily as happy ones. "Until Phyllis came into the family, I hadn't realized how much I missed having a mom—biological or not. With Phyllis, I got the mother I badly needed. That doesn't mean we didn't ever argue over things—like my curfew, for example. But, by and large, we had a great relationship.

"I remember once, after discussing genes in my high

school health class, I asked Phyllis if she thought I had inherited a certain trait of hers. Imagine, I had forgotten we weren't biologically related."

"Mom was laid-back and soft-spoken, but she was firm. All of us kids knew we couldn't make her into a doormat. While I wouldn't consider Mom strict, compared to the years I lived without a mother, she was stern and definitely not a yes-person.

"Since Randy and Laurie maintained their distance toward Phyllis, they were bothered that I confided most in her and that I felt close to my stepbrothers. Maybe they were annoyed, too, that by the time I was thirteen I stopped visiting our mother. Those visits just got to be too much for me. Whatever, my family had a saying: 'Blood is thicker than water—except for Bonnie.' "

Seven and a half years after she became their stepmother, Phyllis died of cancer. She had been sick for years, but none of the children knew how seriously. "Terry was six then, and I was a freshman in college. What a loss for everyone. Two years later Dad married Joyce, a woman with four kids of her own. Again a new family was formed, even larger than the first and second. Last week at the Thanksgiving table, we were forty-three people, counting the parents, children, and grandchildren."

Today Bonnie is married, works as a part-time accountant, and has two children. "I try to be the kind of mother Phyllis was to me—fair and psychologically wise. My stepmother's my role model. Even now, more than twenty years later, I find little fault with her."

Despite Bonnie's strong positive feelings about being in a stepfamily, it still pains her to think about her parents' divorce. "No one wins with divorce, and kids probably suffer the most. My parents' marital breakup was awful for me. But if I had to live with them in an unhappy home, it would have been equally horrible. Maybe the pain I had before Dad's remarriage helped me to appreciate what came after. Anyhow, it taught me that life isn't perfect. It's too bad that I had to learn that lesson so young."

Looking back, Bonnie thinks her and Phyllis's combined families made the ideal household. "I never saw the two families living under the same roof as *we* and *they*. Of course, this didn't happen overnight. It took time for us to grow as a family and to learn to respect one another. We had fun. More important, we were loved. Is there anything else better than that?"

OLIVIA AGE 11

*"When kids ask what my mother does,
I say, 'Which mother?' "*

"With my parents' custody arrangement, I get to see both of them often, so I don't miss either one too much. But because it's an unusual setup, it takes a lot of explaining. A few days ago I went to a friend's, who's also a stepchild. The girl's mother asked me when I see my parents, so I gave her all the details. 'Tell me that another time,' she said. I thought, Oh, no! Here we go again!

"My parents separated when I was almost four and divorced when I was five. Since the separation, my younger sister, Eugenia, and I have spent every Thursday and every other weekend at Mom's. On alternate Wednesdays my sister and I take turns staying at Mom's so we can have time alone with her. All other days we live with Dad."

When Olivia was starting third grade, her father married Christie. Even after the remarriage, Olivia's visiting arrangements stayed the same. Her father bought a larger house so Olivia, Eugenia, and Christie's daughter, Kate, could have their own bedrooms. Olivia's mother's own home is nearby.

"Now the explanations of my life are even more complicated. When kids ask what my mother does, I say, 'Which mother?' I can tell from the looks on their faces that they don't know what I'm talking about. Then I describe my stepfamily situation, which leads to more questions. I'm sure people think I'm pretty strange.

"At least I get to see both my parents a lot, and I like being with each of them. At Mom's there're two cats, and at Dad and Christie's there are a canary, three cats, my rabbit, Kate's ferret, and Eugenia's two hamsters."

Olivia was excited when her father told her he was marrying Christie, because she and Kate had been best friends since they were in nursery school. "I had gone to Kate's birthday parties when I was younger, and now we were going to be stepsisters. Whenever my father and her mother met, she and I had fun together.

"Naturally, I thought we would be as close once our parents married. But it didn't happen that way. Before the wedding, I could sense trouble coming when Kate refused to wear the flower girl dress Christie had picked out for her, Eugenia, and me." Then Olivia's father and Christie let the girls choose their own bedrooms. "Both Kate and I wanted the same room—the biggest—and each of us had our mind set on getting it. Usually I'm not that stubborn, but this was very important to me, and I wouldn't give in.

Olivia with her stepsister, Kate (right)

Kate sulked, and she finally gave up. Today that room is mine."

In the beginning, Kate gave Olivia the most headaches. Five months apart in age (Olivia is older), the two girls were in the same grade and, although they had different teachers and different friends, they still saw a lot of each other. "The hardest thing was when we got into arguments. Kate stopped talking to me and acted as if I wasn't there. No matter how I tried to make up, she kept silent. It took a while to get used to her personality. Finally I realized that Kate doesn't like people copying her or doing things exactly the way she does them, but back then I thought she was just plain difficult.

"Truthfully, I admit that when Dad married Christie, I was a bit spoiled and acted grumpy if I couldn't get what I wanted. I think I started acting like that after the divorce. On the days I lived with Dad, baby-sitters watched me until he came home from work. They gave me as many treats as I asked for. By the time I became part of a stepfamily, I had been used to getting my way.

"So when Christie said, 'No sweets in the house,' I was angry. And later on, when she suggested I switch bedrooms with Kate for a while to make it fair, I wouldn't bend. Nobody was going to force me out of that room!"

In school Olivia's teacher felt that she could benefit from being part of a counseling group with other children. "I was very shy then—in fact, I sat at my desk most of the day and hardly said a word. I can understand why my teacher was concerned. Every week or so, I went to the group meetings, but I had trouble explaining my family situation. Being taken out of class was even worse. It made me feel weird.

"But now I'm much better about telling people what's on my mind. Mostly I speak to Mom 'cause she knows how to make me feel good. Still, I have no difficulty confiding in Christie as long as the problems have nothing to do with her or Kate. And I love talking to Dad. Usually before I go to sleep, he comes into my room and describes the cases he's handled during the day. Dad's a lawyer and tells good stories.

"Since I've been able to talk to someone when I'm unhappy, I feel so much better. Luckily, I have a lot of people whom I feel close to, and we're learning to get along with each other.

"While it's not easy being in a stepfamily, and I wish my parents hadn't divorced, I feel that, if they were unhappy with each other, their marriage had to end.

"What's funny is that I don't ever remember them fighting. Maybe their divorce had more to do with Mom wanting to work full-time and be independent. For some reason she thought she couldn't do that while she was married to Dad. At least I know that I wasn't the cause of their problems."

While she's happy seeing both of her parents so frequently, Olivia says the back-and-forth arrangements still complicate her life. "Whenever I'm at one parent's house, I think I'm missing out on something special that's going on at the other parent's. It's really hard if I'm the only kid away for the day. A few Wednesdays ago when I slept at

Olivia with her parents, stepmother, sister, and stepsisters.
Back row: Christie, Dad, Mom. Front row:
Eugenia, Kate, and Olivia.

Mom's, Christie took Kate and Eugenia to dinner and rented a movie I had wanted to see. The next Wednesday when Eugenia went to Mom's, the two of them saw the firemen's parade and Eugenia got cotton candy. Was I jealous!

"But I like going to Mom's house, since it's quiet there, and she's not at all demanding. That's not to say that Mom doesn't have rules. Eugenia and I have our own chores there.

"And since Christie's not one to fuss much about cleanliness, at Dad's we don't have to worry most of the time when things aren't perfect. Sometimes, however, Christie goes on a neatness kick and gets annoyed if a pencil's out of place or someone's jacket is not hung up. Then I wish I was with Mom. I start thinking, 'Why couldn't my family have been normal and stayed together like it started out?'

"So being in a stepfamily has its good and bad moments. There are so many people with different moods and ways of doing things. But if it has to be, kids shouldn't make a big deal out of it. You get nowhere when you blame your problems on the fact that your parents divorced."

Now that Olivia and Kate are older and more used to living together, they get along better. "If Kate's angry at me, she writes her feelings down in her diary. I like that more than being ignored. Believe it or not, we actually have fun together—playing tag, reading in each other's room, or telling secrets to each other that we don't want the parents to hear.

"Still, I think a family would be better off with no step-people in it. Although I like being in a stepfamily for greedy reasons—I get double the amount of gifts on holidays and celebrate two birthday parties—it's easier for kids, and adults, too, if parents don't divorce. Of course, then everyone must be kind to each other and not act grumpy. That's how I'd like to live."

KATE

"If I'd had my way,
Mom and Dad would have learned
to stop arguing so they could
have stayed together"

"When I was two and a half my parents separated. A year later they divorced. Before Mom remarried, I kind of liked having her to myself—going shopping together, or playing catch and board games. During that time we weren't rich, but with Dad helping us out we weren't poor, either. We lived in a cozy little house that had two bedrooms and one bathroom. It was so cute that I wished I could have stayed there forever. But when I was eight and Mom and Bob got married, I had to move to the larger house they bought. Although it was in the same town, we changed neighborhoods. I couldn't walk to see my friends anymore. Other than that, the idea of Mom marrying Bob was fine with me. Our families had spent a lot of time together and I had fun with Bob's two girls.

"Later on, though, I found out that it was one thing to

play with Eugenia and Olivia, and another to live with them. Being in the same house with my stepsisters isn't always that easy. Only now am I realizing what Mom's remarriage really means."

In the beginning Kate was confused by all the changes. Instead of telling people what made her unhappy, she just went along with things. "I especially remember the day Olivia, Eugenia, and I picked our own rooms. The three of us went upstairs, and Olivia immediately claimed the largest room for herself. I got mad 'cause I wanted that room, too, but I didn't argue much for it. Back then, I gave in right away but sulked a lot.

"Another thing that bothered me was that Olivia kept copying whatever I did. When I chose pink and white curtains for my windows, she asked Mom to buy them for her, too. It got so that I couldn't even use my favorite expressions, like 'dah hickey,' without Olivia or Eugenia saying them also.

"Finally, as a way to let them know how annoyed I was, I started writing in my diary while they were in my room. Olivia was particularly curious to know what I was saying, and naturally I wouldn't tell her. After a while, she got the point, and now her copying me is no longer a problem."

Since her mother's remarriage, Kate has thought a lot about her relationship with her stepsisters and with her remarried father's young son, Coleman. Coleman's link to her is confusing. "I only see my half-brother every other weekend when I visit Dad and his wife, Ann. But because we share the same father, that makes him part of my *real* family. Although I'm with Olivia and Eugenia much more, we're not related, so that makes them sort of friends. Yet if I had to answer quickly, I'd call them my sisters.

"While we mostly get along okay, we have big fights, too, and for me, that's the worst thing. It just doesn't seem right that sisters should behave that way.

"All the years I lived alone with Mom there was only her to argue with, and we didn't disagree that much. So fighting with my stepsisters is something new to me. Luckily, Mom listens to me and understands what I'm talking about. More than anyone, she knows how to make me feel better. Dad understands, too, but I'm not with him that much to tell him what's going on."

Kate has also had to adjust to being the middle child in the family. "As an only child for eight years, I was the oldest and youngest at the same time. Now I'm neither. What really bothers me is that Olivia and I are only five months apart, but those few months mean a lot to people, including my mother and stepfather. They assume that because of this small age difference, Olivia is the more responsible of the two of us. Recently, Mom and Bob went out for dinner and left Olivia in charge of Eugenia and me. With all my experience taking care of Coleman, they should have made me the baby-sitter instead!

"Being the middle sister was especially hard for me when Eugenia was very little. Everyone babied her. 'Isn't she cute?' they'd say. Then, when she got older, they'd comment on how much she had grown. Because of Eugenia, people barely noticed me. Not that Eugenia's nine, it's

*Kate, center, with Olivia, top,
and Eugenia, right.*

much less of a problem, but I still don't like it in the middle.

"Of all things that upset me as a stepchild, though, the worst is knowing my family life will never be the same again. The hardest part is the constant going from one parent's house to the next. Half the time I'm not sure where I'll be. For a while I used to say yes to party invitations and forget I was going to be at Dad's house that weekend. Now Dad tells me to accept no matter what, and he picks me up afterward."

Olivia and Eugenia also come and go. "One day the girls are here and the next day they're not. For me, at least, there's an advantage. When Olivia and Eugenia stay at their mom's, I get a chance to be alone with Bob and my mother.

"Bob and I are friends and enjoy joking around. Sometimes he surprises me with gifts like T-shirts and notebooks. When I was younger, Bob told me he was Superman. Deep down I didn't believe him, but still I kept asking how he could fly and lift heavy things.

"While Bob's very nice, he's not perfect—especially when he nags me, like other people I won't mention. Also, he can be strict. At the dinner table, he insists we kids have good manners.

"When it was just Mom and me in the house, we mostly ate our meals off snack tables. I never put my napkin on my lap, and I had no idea that my elbows belonged at my side. Now we eat in the dining room, by candlelight, using my great-grandmother's china plates. Every night Mom cooks something special, like chicken with sauce, or pasta. Considering how awful we could behave, Eugenia, Olivia, and I act pretty good."

Kate's dad only lives a half hour away from her now, so it's not a big trip for her to see him. "Whenever I go to his house, we have fun just hanging out or doing real special things, like going to the circus. Last week I spent the day at his office, and he took me around to meet the artists who work for him. One of them was designing wrappers for bubble gum and cotton candy and tried to teach me to draw cartoon characters. I did a rotten job.

"My grandparents, too, treat me special, but they live far away. Even though they're very nice to Olivia and Eugenia, I always know I'm their favorite. Eugenia and Olivia's grandma—Bob's mother—acts the same with her grandchildren. If she's on a trip and sends everyone postcards, she'll write words from top to bottom to Olivia and Eugenia, and only one short sentence to me.

"One thing I worried about when Mom remarried was whether I would get the same amount of attention with two more kids in the house. It's amazing how Mom makes time for all of us. Since she married Bob, I've never felt neglected. As soon as I asked her to help me with my science project, she was there to give me support. Mostly I do well in school, but once in a while Bob gives me a hand with my work. Truthfully, I like it better when he takes me skiing."

Because Kate and Olivia are in the same grade and taking the same subjects, they often get the same homework. "While I sometimes wish Olivia wasn't in my school—especially after we've had a fight—in the end it works out fine for both of us. If I have a problem with something in school, Olivia explains it to me, and I do that for her, too.

That's an advantage of having a stepsister your own age."

The longer her mother and Bob are married, the more Kate likes her stepfamily. "While we're not really related and we don't look alike, I'm sure that, to outsiders, we seem pretty normal together. At home, too, we act like a regular family, although we don't even have the same last names. For that matter, neither do my mother and I, anymore. Of all things, somehow I mind that the least.

"Still, I wish Mom and Dad could be back with each other. That's what I want most. They're my real family. I don't like that one part of my family is here and another is somewhere else. But no way would it be worth living with them if I had to hear fights, and that's what I'm most afraid would happen.

"If I'd had my way, Mom and Dad would have learned to stop arguing so they could have stayed together. Then we'd be one family, as it's supposed to be."

As for giving advice to other children in stepfamilies, Kate hesitates. "I don't want to sound like a therapist. Actually, I stopped going to a therapist who was supposed to help me get along better with Olivia and Eugenia because I didn't like someone giving me advice. Besides, solving my own problems is hard enough, so how can I tell anybody else what to do?"

One day Kate plans to become a teacher and to get married. "I want two kids—a boy and a girl. All I can hope for is that, to the very end, my own family stays as it originally started out—with the same mother and father."

· ·

SCOTT A. AGE 8½

*"I wasn't sure which home
was my real one anymore, or where I belonged"*

"I was only two and a half when my parents separated, so I don't remember much of what went on. Even now, I'm not exactly sure why my parents stopped living together. They say it's because they married too young. I think it's because they were tired of each other."

Either way, divorce is a subject Scott doesn't like to discuss. When he was five and his mother tried to explain it to him again, he covered his ears and wouldn't listen. "All I knew was that Dad wasn't coming home any more, which really made me angry and was also confusing.

"When Dad left he moved into his own apartment not too far away. I liked it, because it was so different from the big house that Mom and I stayed in.

"Every Saturday when I came for the weekend Dad and I did errands first. Then we went to the park where Dad

97

pushed me on the swings or played catch with me. Early on Sunday morning I'd wake him up by running into his room and climbing into his bed. After we were dressed, we'd go out to buy the paper and doughnuts."

Two years after the divorce, Scott's father married Amy. They moved to a house, and now they have a nine-month-old baby named Lindsey. Since then, Scott hasn't been able to run into his father's room on Sunday mornings. "Dad says I have to stay quiet until nine-thirty. Especially now, with Lindsey, he and Amy need their rest. I miss the way it used to be when it was just Dad and me. Now there's no doughnut shop near his house. Once in a while, though, the four of us have breakfast in a restaurant and I get to order waffles. It's lots of fun, but it's not the same as it was."

A year and a half ago, Scott's mother also remarried. His stepfather, Rob, had custody of his own two daughters, Dori, thirteen and a half, and Nikki, fifteen. After being an only child for seven years, Scott now has two stepsisters, as well as his half-sister, Lindsey. "When Mom told me she was marrying Rob, I cheered and told her, 'I love that man.' I was also excited about having Dori and Nikki as my stepsisters.

"Rob and the girls lived in my town, and I'd known them since Mom started dating Rob when I was about five. I remember our families getting together for dinner every Sunday when we three kids got home from visiting our other parents. One time the girls and I returned early, and Rob surprised us by taking everyone apple-picking. Then we went to his house and made a pie. Rob cored the apples, Dori and Nikki peeled and piled them into the shell, I sprinkled them with cinnamon, and Mom cleaned up the mess. That was a great day, and the pie was delicious.

"A little while later, I started thinking about all the changes that would come with Mom's remarriage, and suddenly I was worried. It had taken me a while to get used to being at Dad's after he married Amy. Now I was finally comfortable in his house and felt part of his family. And I liked the way Mom and I did things together, too. But when I thought about Rob coming into my family, and *more* changes, I became mad.

"Although Mom explained that, because Rob was moving into our house, I could stay in the same neighborhood and school, I still felt awful. I wasn't sure which home was my real one anymore, or where I belonged.

"That wasn't the only problem. I was afraid of what living with Rob would be like. Although I liked being with him and he was real nice, he was much stricter than Mom. With Mom, if I did something wrong, she gave me lots of chances to change my behavior before she punished me. But I noticed when the two families were together that Rob made Dori and Nikki follow his rules right away."

Anticipating Nikki and Dori in his house also made Scott anxious. Would his mother have enough time for him? "Mom told me the girls would be staying with us only until their mother got settled into a job and a place to live. Then they would move in with her. Still, I didn't know when that would be.

"All I could think of was Mom carpooling every minute

for Dori and Nikki. And every time she drove the girls someplace I had to come along, which meant I couldn't play with my friend Matt."

The more Scott considered his mother's forthcoming marriage, the angrier he became. Soon he was losing his temper over the least little thing. "There was too much going on at one time, and I didn't like it. Finally, Mom took me to a therapist, because I was screaming too much. I went to him for a few months before Mom and Rob married and kept going for a couple of months after that. I'm not sure how, but the therapist helped me control my yelling when things didn't go exactly the way I wanted.

"Anyhow, when we all started living together, it wasn't as bad as I expected. In fact, when Nikki and Dori left to join their mother six months later, I missed them. I liked having them around when I came home from school, especially if they baby-sat me when Mom was running errands. Also, we had great times putting on shows.

"Still, I enjoy the peace of being an only child. I know that sisters and brothers argue, but I couldn't get used to that part. Every time Dori or Nikki slammed her bedroom door and said I couldn't come in, I became furious. And I hated when the two of them raced into the car to sit together so I couldn't be in the middle.

"Now I kind of like having the house to myself. That way I don't have to share my stereo and tapes as I do when Dori and Nikki spend every other weekend here. Also, Mom makes sure Matt comes over more often so I won't be lonely."

Since the girls are gone, Scott has more time alone with

Rob, too. "Recently he taught me 'Chopsticks' on the piano, which I now know by heart. Both Rob and I like soft rock and baseball, too. Way back, when I was younger, he taught me to pitch and catch so I would be in good shape for the Little League tryouts. Everytime I was ready to give up, he encouraged me to keep going.

"But what I was afraid of in the beginning, about rules and Rob, has turned out to be true. All of a sudden, Matt and I can't run around the house the way we used to. Both Mom and Rob tell us to keep down the noise. Once Mom even sent Matt home when we didn't listen. Since she married Rob, Mom's stricter."

At the dinner table particularly, Rob expects Scott to behave well. "If I leave the table before asking to be excused or finishing my meal, Rob makes me sit down again until he says it's time to go. Then I have to bring my plate into the kitchen, something Mom never cared about when it was just the two of us.

"At Dad's house, I also have more chores. It's not that I'm older and I'm being told to do more. If it was up to Dad, I'd be totally free. But Amy, who's even stricter than Mom, says I must make my bed every day. Also she insists I wash my hands before dinner and she corrects the way I sit at the table, although she doesn't mind that the baby makes a mess with her food.

"All these people telling me what to do sometimes gets on my nerves. And the different rules in the two houses can be confusing. At Dad's, I can wander down to the train station by myself, but at Mom's I have to stay close to home.

She won't allow me to go to other kids' houses unless she takes me there.

"Still, I'm lucky that all the people in my family are nice to me. Last time I was at Dad's, Amy and I made a pumpkin pie. It was probably the best I ever had.

"And Dad's still my buddy. Now that Amy's busy taking care of the baby, he and I have more time to go off by ourselves. We take his car, which we named the Grady Ghost, and drive to stores to buy tapes and posters for me. Because of the way we hang around together, Dad calls us the Two Musketeers."

Last summer, Scott and his father went to Washington, D.C., for almost a week. It was the first long vacation in years that Scott had had with just his dad. "Both of us brought our cameras on the trip and took photos of each other. My favorite is a shot of Dad relaxing in bed, and he has a funny one of me sitting on a park bench, tired and hot."

Sometimes Scott misses his father and wishes his mom and dad were back together again. Other times he says that being in a stepfamily has its advantages, especially on holidays and birthdays. "If Halloween comes on the weekend, I first trick-or-treat at my house, then go around Dad's neighborhood and get more candy. On Christmas, I celebrate with Mom, then go to Dad's and get more presents. Since Rob's Jewish, we celebrate Chanukah, too—more gifts. And because of him, we're invited to Passover seders, which I like. Of course, birthdays mean more toys and two cakes.

"But what I like best about being a stepchild is having a larger family. I love when Rob's father visits and we play ball together. And it's fun doing things with Mom and Rob when Dori and Nikki are along. Last summer, Rob took us tubing down a river and we had a terrific time. Luckily, I was in the same tube as Rob, because the current was really strong."

When Scott thinks about the future, he hopes he'll have a wife who will spend a lot of time doing things with him. And he plans to have a family, too. "I'll make sure the mother and father stay together. It's easier for kids if their parents don't divorce. Since I like both of my parents, it's harder living with only one most of the time. Right now I think I belong with Mom, but one day when I'm older I might want to stay with Dad. More than anything, I wish I could see him every day.

"At least he doesn't live that far away, and we're good friends. Now that he has cable television and I don't, it's more exciting to go to his house. Being in a stepfamily has its problems, but whichever house I go to, I'm happy there. So, for me, being a stepchild isn't that bad."

SCOTT AGE 19

"I've tried to accept what can't be"

"For the first nine years of my life, Dad traveled weekdays on business and came home on weekends. Every Saturday morning, I couldn't wait to run into his room to wake him. One morning, though, he wasn't there. When I asked Mom and my two older sisters, Jill and Missy, what was going on, they said he had stayed out. Truthfully, my parents had separated, but nobody wanted to tell me. Looking back, the day Dad left was the saddest day of my life."

For the next year, Scott's father came home for dinner now and then and visited on weekends, but Scott rarely knew far in advance when this would happen. "The bottom line was that I saw Dad much less than I ever had, and I finally asked him why. Dad blamed his absence on longer business trips, but I knew something else was wrong.

"For one thing, Mom was the angriest I had ever seen

her. She took out her bad feelings by drinking, and by hitting me and my older sister Missy. For some reason, Jill was spared. Although hitting us was nothing new with Mom, it now happened more frequently.

"Besides hitting me, Mom punished me for minor things. For example, she knew how much I loved being with Dad, especially on weekends when he got baseball tickets, but she'd ground me for some trouble I'd caused during the week and wouldn't let me go. No matter how much Dad tried to change her mind, she wouldn't bend."

His parents' poor relationship, however, was something Scott had always lived with. In fact, Scott can't remember a time when they *didn't* argue. "It wasn't a happy home for my sisters and me to grow up in. So when Mom told me a year after Dad left that they were getting divorced, I thought, Good, that's the way it should be.

"Then I started worrying about who I'd be living with. For as long as my sisters were at home, I had allies. Through the years, my sisters sometimes helped to get me off the hook with Mom by taking the blame for things I'd done. Of course, that didn't always work. Once my mother gave me a black and blue ear. But at least I felt better knowing Jill and Missy were close by. All of a sudden, though, Missy was going off to college and Jill would be leaving soon, too. With the divorce news, I finally realized that Dad was never coming back. I wondered who in the house could protect me."

Then Scott's mother astonished him by asking which parent he wanted to live with. "This took me by surprise.

I quickly mumbled, 'Dad,' immediately worrying that I had hurt her. 'Well, that's that,' Mom said. 'You'll live with your father, and I don't want to hear another word about it.' In my mind, a miracle had occurred."

The day Scott moved out, he was cool to his mom. "As I walked towards the door to leave with Dad, she shouted, 'Don't ever forget I'm your mother.' Those words have stayed with me ever since.

"From Mom's house we drove straight to Anne's. She was the woman Dad was living with, and her home was now to be mine, too. I had met Anne once, when I was about eight. Other than that, I knew nothing about her, except that her house was not far from my mother's.

"The more I thought about moving in with her, the more nervous I got. On the one hand, I was happy to be leaving Mom. On the other, I had no idea what Anne—a stranger— was like. Even though she and Dad were not married, I thought of her as a stepmother. And, having only heard bad things about stepmothers, I imagined Anne to be the Wicked Witch of the West. Worse, she had never been married and had no experience with kids. But, I thought, at least she was willing to take me in, and that said some-thing positive about her."

From the beginning, Anne tried hard to prove to Scott and his father that she could be a good mother. And there was immediate evidence that she was. "What was inter-esting was how quickly my grades improved once I moved in. After doing miserably for years, I began to catch on to things. And I made friends. While living at Mom's, my sisters and I mostly hung around together, never inviting kids over or going to their houses. After I was at Anne's, these things changed for me.

"Also, I was thankful to be living with her and Dad. With them together, I felt like I was in a real family, and in a better situation than if Dad and I had just lived alone."

Still, there were adjustments Scott had to make. "Anne's firm rules about how she wanted the family to act in the house were quite different from the way I had been brought up. This really bothered me. When I was with my mother and wanted to get out of a bad situation, I packed a knapsack with Oreo cookies and ran away to a field not far from my house. Then, I could count on one of my sisters to bring me back. But now, alone, I had to handle my problems differently.

"Mostly I shouted at Anne when I was angry. She and I usually fought over my messy habits and her insistence on neatness. The more she nagged me to pick up my stuff, the more I razzed her, until we were locked in a power struggle which lasted, on and off, for years. Often I was tempted to say to her, 'Don't tell me what to do. You're not my mother.' But I knew how furious Dad would be with me, so I held my tongue. Besides, Anne was sensitive, and deep down, I didn't want to hurt her. After all, she cared about me. If I was sick, she came straight home from work to make sure I was okay. While that's not much to ask of a mother, it's a lot to expect from someone not related."

Scott visited his biological mother every few months, though she urged him to come more often. "I liked seeing Jill, but going home reminded me too much of my past. I knew my infrequent visits hurt Mom, but it was best for me.

"Then Dad was offered a job in another city, so we had to move. Since I hadn't lived that long in Anne's neighborhood, leaving wasn't such a big deal. As it turned out, the next two years were among the happiest of my life. I made close friends, Keith and David, the first real buddies I ever had. We played football together, slept at one another's houses, or just had fun hanging out. In school, I continued to do well. I finally felt as if the sun was shining through.

"About this time, Mom wrote me a letter, which arrived on my birthday. In it she described her hard life: marrying Dad as a teenager, and then having Missy right away. She told me how difficult finances had always been for them and how miserable she was raising the kids alone, with Dad first going to college and holding two part-time jobs, and later being on the road so much. In more ways than one, my mother asked me to forgive her." But being only twelve, with his past still fresh in his mind, Scott wasn't ready to tell his mother that he understood her difficulties.

"Not long after I received Mom's letter, Dad was offered an even better position in another state, and we had to move again. When I heard about this move, I was heartbroken. 'How can you take me away from my friends, now that I've settled in?' I asked. It took me almost a month to get rid of my anger. The worst was saying good-bye to Keith and David. It was a traumatic day for the three of us. We were so choked up, we couldn't talk.

"At least I looked forward to the house that Anne, Dad,

and I had picked out in the suburbs. And I liked the school when I visited it beforehand. As a bonus, we'd now be an hour away from New York City, which seemed exciting, too.

"But from the moment I walked into my eighth grade class, I knew the kids weren't going to be friendly. Other than Seth, a boy who lived two houses away, no one was nice to me. Until tenth grade, I had a hard time being accepted. My grades went down, and I started drinking.

"Finally, one of my teachers referred me to the school psychologist, who recommended I join a counseling group with other kids my age. In those sessions, with the psychologist in charge, we talked about things that were causing us problems—alcohol, drugs, divorce, and living with a stepparent."

One of the biggest issues for Scott was learning not to be afraid of people. "After living with my mother for ten years and being scared, I had difficulty trusting anybody. Whenever I met someone new, I immediately thought they were out to get me. It didn't matter if it was Anne, her family, or my teachers.

"Naturally, with this attitude, things had to go wrong. I'd get in trouble and then blame myself, thinking I was the bad one. Even as a kid, I'd thought it was my fault when my sisters got into a tiff with Mom.

"At least I didn't believe that I caused my parents' divorce. For whatever reason, I knew it was their problem."

Today, Scott feels that the group meetings with the school psychologist helped him to be more open with others and to trust people. "In time, I became friends with three

. . . .

of the guys who were also in the sessions. Now, besides
Seth, I had others I could turn to. After that, I started
working on getting my life together."

Meanwhile, six months after the second move, Scott's
father and Anne were married. "To me the marriage was
just a matter of course. Whatever they wanted was fine as
long as I could keep living with them. I didn't have to have
Anne as my legal stepmother to know how much I meant
to her. She had proven that to my sisters and me through
the years.

"We kids had to grow up to accept her, and although it
took us some time, Anne never gave up on us. Despite our
being suspicious of her and challenging what she said,
Anne always cared. If she went on trips, she brought us
back gifts. She let my sisters live with us for months as
they got established in college or in jobs. And now that I'm
in college, she calls to see how I'm doing."

Looking back, Scott believes immaturity was not the sole
cause of his wariness of Anne. Having been physically
abused by his mother made him fearful and cautious of
nearly everyone—including his own father. "As a kid, I
knew Dad loved me. He never hit or yelled, and he tried
to do things to make me happy. Still, I couldn't understand
why he stayed away from home so much. For years, I
thought I was the reason.

"I had to live with my father on a daily basis to see how
much I meant to him. Today he's the one I go to for advice
about school or a job. While we don't always agree, I know
he has my interests at heart."

Despite the positive feelings that Scott has about his

stepfamily, he still wishes his mother and father could have worked their marriage out. "My mother and father made a lot of mistakes back then. Now that I'm older, I'm better able to appreciate how hard they had it, and I can forgive both of them. That's all in the past and can't be corrected. I've tried to accept what can't be—that's life—but I can't help but think about the possibilities, especially since Mom has changed so much in the last ten years. Now that she's no longer angry at Dad, she's calmer and more caring. When I visited about six months ago, I noticed she didn't yell once. Even her house has improved. She keeps the inside neat and has planted a beautiful flower garden outdoors. At college, I call Mom from time to time. She's a good listener, particularly if I'm having problems with Dad or a girlfriend. Remembering how she was and what she's like today, I think, This lady is great. While I don't visit her that often and feel badly about it, our relationship is certainly better than it used to be.

"But Anne is understanding, too. I find it very easy to talk to her. When we first lived together and I complained about Dad, she refused to get in the middle of things. But now, if she thinks I'm right, she'll talk to Dad and present my side of the story. So I have a bunch of adults to go to.

"Last month Missy was married, and the three parents came to the wedding. When I saw Mom sitting at the table with Dad's family, I couldn't believe it. Nobody would have predicted that years back."

All in all, Scott feels that he's come out ahead with his father's remarriage. But looking back, he thinks his parents

. . . .

could have handled their separation and divorce better. "For one, there should have been definite custody arrangements so I wasn't the one to make the choice. From the start, I knew I wanted to live with Dad, but I've always felt guilty about hurting Mom, in spite of what she did. Also, we kids should have been told right away why our parents were divorcing.

"Dad should have made sure that Anne and I felt comfortable with each other before I moved into her house. He could have taken us out for dinner a few times and then gradually explained that the three of us would be living as a family. Maybe that way, I would have been less confused.

"Until I moved in with Anne and Dad, I was positive I'd never get married or have kids. I worried that I might be hard on my wife and children because of my abuse experience. Fortunately, I lived with Anne and Dad long enough to appreciate how much they love each other. Anne became the mother I needed. I owe it to her that we became a family again. I was lucky to get a nice stepmother."

Scott's advice to other kids in stepfamilies is to always have hope. "I never thought my life could get better, but it did. With time and patience, I'm finally having good times.

"Now, as I look into the future, there is so much pointing to my success."

GABE AGE 23

"Kids and stepparents need to be tolerant of one another"

"My parents separated when I was three, but I usually think of that time as being when their divorce took place. To me, divorce and separation are the same. Because I was too young to understand what was going on, I've since asked Mom and Dad why their marriage didn't work out. Each said that years back they loved each other, but it wasn't the kind of love that gets people through difficult times in life."

Following the breakup of his parent's marriage, Gabe lived with his mother while his father lived in an apartment nearby. "Every other weekend I stayed at Dad's, and one night a week he came to take me out for dinner. When I got older, we went to the movies or bowling, which I loved.

"Fortunately, my mother was a structured person who liked routines. At home, dinner was served at a certain time and holidays were celebrated in a specific way. From the moment she and Dad separated, they set up definite visiting arrangements so I always knew when I'd be with him. This scheduling added consistency to my life and made me feel more stable.

"Although I enjoyed the visits with my dad, in general I must have been very unhappy. Mom told me that in first grade I often came home from school crying. Finally she brought me to the Jewish Family Service, which matched me with Doug. Twice a week, Doug picked me up from school and we did things together. He's the one who taught me to bowl. Doug was not only a counselor, he was a big brother to me, too."

On the afternoons when Gabe didn't see Doug, he had a music lesson or went to Hebrew school. There he met his future stepfather. "Daniel led the Junior Congregation at synagogue, and whenever Mom came to get me she'd see him, but they didn't date until later. So I knew Daniel before she did. Once he and Mom started going out, they saw a lot of each other, and gradually Mom brought him more into my life. Some evenings she invited Daniel for supper or we visited him at his house. After a while, he slept over on Friday nights, since he didn't ride on the Sabbath and he wanted to be with us. Because of him, Mom started making Shabbat dinner, which was something new in our house."

On Saturdays when Daniel had stayed over, Gabe and he got up early and walked to synagogue. That was their special time together. "I loved sitting next to Daniel in synagogue, watching the men look so cool as they prayed. Best was when there was a Bar Mitzvah, and the women in the balcony threw candies at the boys. To this day, I owe my Jewish soul to my stepfather.

"When I was in third grade, Daniel told me that he and Mom were getting married. I didn't think it was such a big deal, since he already hung out with us so much. Still, there were some things about the remarriage which concerned me. For one, I didn't know what to call him. Daniel said to say whatever made me feel comfortable. So I called him Danny Yell, the way I thought it was pronounced in Hebrew.

"Another problem was not liking how Mom and he acted together. During the years it was just her and me, Mom always came into my room to kiss me good-night. Now that she was affectionate with Daniel, too, I was jealous."

Not long after his mother remarried, the family moved to Israel so Daniel could study there for a year. "Leaving my school and neighborhood wasn't a problem to me since I knew I was going to return. The worst thing was being far away from Dad. We were very close, and it bothered me that I wouldn't see him for so long.

"Mom understood how upset I was and set things up so that every Sunday night I talked to Dad on the phone. Also, Dad and I sent tapes back and forth to keep each other posted."

This was typical of how his parents worked together whenever an issue came up that involved Gabe's welfare. "Although their marriage had ended, they still kept in touch, especially when it came to making serious decisions about me. Daniel was part of these plans, too. He and Dad got along, which made things easier. With his knack for calming people, Daniel helped reduce tension in the family, particularly when a crunch time came, like my Bar Mitzvah. If it wasn't for him, I'm not sure that day would have turned out so well, with my parents standing next to me on the bimah and Daniel as the rabbi.

"The longer I lived with my stepfather, the more attached we became. Soon I realized he was playing a second fatherly role in my life, without trying to take my dad's place. In fact, Daniel did just the opposite; he always supported my relationship with my father. And he never interfered with my special time with Mom.

"As for disciplining me, Mom handled that. If I got poor grades or sneaked in to watch TV, she was the one who grounded me. Of course, Daniel reprimanded me if something came up at the moment, but luckily I was an easy kid, so I didn't get in much trouble."

From the time his mother remarried, Gabe begged her to have a baby. "I wanted a brother and couldn't have one fast enough. Daniel and Mom wanted to wait until he became a rabbi and had his own pulpit. So, four and a half years after their marriage, Mom became pregnant. I was ecstatic, especially when the test showed she would have a boy. Nothing could have pleased me more. Today, almost eleven years later, I still consider my brother Ari's birth one of the best things to happen in my life. Later, when my sister, Marissa, and brother Misha were born, it was even better."

Although Ari was Daniel's natural son, Gabe never

wished he was his stepfather's biological child, too. "I was happy with my dad, and got annoyed when people mistakenly sent me mail using Daniel's last name. On the other hand, I felt uncomfortable when people at synagogue asked how I was related to the rabbi. Instead of telling them the truth, I said I was his son. Somehow the word 'stepchild' made me feel funny."

When Gabe was in high school, Daniel got an appealing offer to lead another synagogue in a different state, and he decided to take advantage of it. "Although I wasn't crazy about where we lived, I was tired of being uprooted and hated having to change my life again. Yet I adjusted quickly to the new area, which was definitely an improvement. Also, I liked the high school and had no trouble making friends.

"As a teenager, I had my share of confrontations with Daniel. Most stemmed from things like how to take care of a car and how clean or dirty a house should be. At least Daniel never bugged me about my room. My room was *my* room, and even today I keep it the way I like.

"But there were plenty of other subjects Daniel and I locked horns on, mainly because he wouldn't budge from his point of view. This frustrated me to no end."

Although Gabriel found it hardest to get along with Daniel during his teenage years, he admits that his stepfather's steadiness and solidity helped to smooth over these rough times. "Despite his being stubborn now and then, Daniel has an open mind and understands my needs. If I have trouble making a decision, he separates the large issues from the small ones. As a young kid I mostly went to

Mom with my problems, but I always knew Daniel was there for me, too. Now that I'm older and have graduated college, I turn to him more and more for advice.

"Today I realize that there's a lot of Daniel in me, namely, his sense of humor and ideas on morality. Sometimes Mom laughs when she hears me say things that sound as if they've come out of Daniel's mouth. Like Daniel, I'm a mediator. If two people have a problem, I'm pretty good at helping them get out of it."

Now that he's older, Gabe thinks he understands why some stepfamily situations work out and others don't. "Kids and stepparents need to be tolerant of one another, especially in the beginning. Both the adult and the child are so scared of everything new. That's why children shouldn't pass judgment on a stepparent until they understand that person. If children never give their stepparents a chance, they can mess things up for the whole family.

"These days, I feel very good about the family I'm in. More and more, I'm aware how much my stepfamily has enhanced me. Last weekend, I went home, and as I played ball with Ari I thought, Now I have what I dreamed about. In my mind, Ari's not my stepbrother or my half-brother. He's *my brother*!

"As a little kid, I might have wished my mom and dad had stayed together, but as an adult, I see they don't mix well. With my solid stepfather, my grandparents to whom I'm very attached, and my good relationship with Dad, I have a strong family. If Daniel's family had lived nearby, I know I would have been close with them, too.

"When I was much younger, I once asked Mom if she

thought Daniel might leave us and she told me, 'I'm going to be married to him for the rest of my life.' On various occasions Daniel too has said, 'I don't know what I'd do without your mother.' Nice!"

Gabe is most thankful that, despite their divorce, both of his parents have taken an active role in his life. "My room-mate's girlfriend hasn't seen her father in years. That's not good for anyone. I think kids benefit if they're connected to their parents. Otherwise, they pay for it later on.

"There was a point when I thought my parents never should have married. That way I wouldn't have gone through all that hard stuff. But then I realized that if they hadn't married, I wouldn't be here. And I'm so glad to be alive."

KARINA AGE 12½

"It's better than ever"

Karina and her brother, Rod, were born in Venezuela, their father's native country. The children's mother, who is American, moved to Venezuela as a child, grew up there, and married. "Dad was married and divorced before he met Mom. Then Mom's and his marriage didn't work out, either. They separated when I was two and a half and Rod was six months old. We stayed in Venezuela until I was seven. Then Mom, Rod, and I moved to the United States.

"Before we left, I saw Dad every week, and sometimes even more. He'd drop by our house to see Rod and me or take us out to lunch and to the beach. Lots of times his two kids from his first marriage came along. They were much older than me, but it didn't matter because we had fun together and I liked them. I'll never forget when Dad took us all to Disney World. We had a ball.

"Of his first two kids, I was closer to Cuchi, my stepsister,

121

who's now eighteen. Even though we don't live near each other anymore, we still keep in touch. Cuchi calls long distance just to talk to me, and I get in touch with her whenever I go to Venezuela to visit Dad and my two grandmothers.

"But since I've moved, I don't see Dad that much. It's expensive for him to travel from Venezuela, and even phone calls cost a lot. Now the only time I visit is when I go to Venezuela for three weeks at Christmas."

In the beginning, the move to the United States was especially difficult for Karina. Not only was she separated from her father and grandparents, but she had to learn a new language, English, attend a new school, and make new friends. "When Mom, Rod, and I came to America we didn't know anyone. Worse, we got an apartment in the city, which I hated. In Venezuela, we lived near the beach, and that was so beautiful. In the city, the only place I could run around was a fenced-in playground.

"To make it harder, we had very little money. Almost as soon as we arrived, Mom started taking courses, but she didn't work for two years. Although Dad sent us money, it was only enough to buy necessities. Whenever I wanted something special, I had to think carefully about the price."

Shortly after Karina's mother began working, the family moved to a suburban area. "In the end, Mom missed the city, but Rod and I didn't. We were much happier in the new place, where we made lots of friends and did well in school.

"Almost immediately after we moved, Mom met Perry at a party. He called her a few times, and then a month later they started dating. At first, Mom didn't introduce Perry to Rod and me. She and Perry would just go out for dinner alone. But when they had known each other about two months, she invited Perry to our house. From then on, he spent every Saturday with the family. Either he'd hang around and the four of us would play baseball, or we'd go to a museum and then to a restaurant. Once he asked us to come to the house he was restoring. We live there now. He let Rod and I paint the walls. I chose red for the downstairs, which is the color it's stayed ever since."

After dating Perry for a year and a half, Karina's mother told the children that she and Perry planned to marry on Valentine's Day. "Although I was happy with the news, because I really liked Perry and he was fun to be with, I was upset when Mom also said we'd be moving again. I thought that surely Perry would have chosen our house over his, since his was in a small, quiet town far from everything. But he needed to be close to where he worked and wanted to be near his parents and brother, who lived a few miles away.

"When Mom saw how miserable I was, she promised she'd take me to visit my friends so I wouldn't lose touch with them. And she said I could call them when I got lonely. Since neither my brother nor I remembered living with our father, Mom also warned us that it might be different having a man in the house. I wasn't so worried about that, because Perry acted more like a friend to Rod and me."

To her surprise, Karina found the move—and the remarriage—easy to handle. "Although the area is totally different from what I was used to, I like my friends here.

Karina and Perry

Another good thing is that I live close to a ski slope and have really gotten into that sport.

"Also, Perry makes things more fun. He's different from most people I know. In his heart he's a big kid. Like Rod and me, he's hooked on heavy metal, and if I ask he'll play my favorite songs on his bass or electric guitar. Sometimes he creates his own words and music. One piece he wrote about the Grand Union supermarket cracked me up. For a while Perry tried to teach me to play guitar, but I was hopeless.

"Besides being musical, Perry paints, sculpts, and makes caricatures. Like him, I'm talented in art. Whenever I want to improve my drawings, I ask him for help. Recently he showed me how to make cartoons. When I told him I'd also like to work with clay, he went out and bought me some."

Seven months ago, Karina's mother had a baby boy. "With Martin in our family, it's better than ever. He's so cute that I don't even mind taking care of him. When Mom and Perry go out, I feed him, change his diapers—ugh—and put him to sleep. The best part is that I get paid for the job.

"Since Perry was never married to anyone before Mom, Rod, Martin, and I are his only kids. Not ever having grandchildren, Perry's parents treat the three of us special. Although I love visiting my relatives in Venezuela, I don't get to see them that much. Now I have a new family: Perry's mother, father, and brother, Matt.

"Still, I think a lot about my grandparents in Venezuela—especially my grandma, Mom's mother. Last time I visited Venezuela, I stayed with her instead of Dad. She makes me feel so good. Soon she's coming to America for a few months, and she will live with us. I can't wait."

As for her biological father, Karina's feelings have cooled—in part because of his remarriage two years ago. "Diane had two kids from another marriage, and then Dad and she had another baby, Eva. Having to support all these new people means Dad has less money to send to Rod and me. While I like Diane a lot, it makes me unhappy that, because she and Dad are together, he's forgetting about his kids in America. It's not only the money part that bothers me. Dad hardly calls me anymore.

"Last Christmas when I saw him, I told him I was angry about how he was treating Rod and me. At the time, he listened and promised things would change. But so far nothing has, and five months have passed.

"Recently I wanted to change my last name to Perry's and stop using Dad's. I think I'm feeling that way because I'm so mad at Dad. In the end, I doubt I'll ever go through with it."

While not happy about her parents' divorce, Karina is now more accepting of the situation. "If parents can't live together, they have to end the marriage whether or not they have kids. Of course, before they give up they should try very hard to work things out.

"Rod and I were lucky that Mom met a man as nice as Perry. It was also good that we spent lots of time with him before they married. That way I could tell Perry was sincere. Some of Mom's other boyfriends pretended they liked Rod and me, but they couldn't fool us.

"To make remarriage easier for the kids, I think it's a good idea for parents to talk to their children beforehand and tell them what changes to expect once the stepparent comes into the family. Also, parents should listen to their kids to find out how *they* feel about the situation. I'm sure the greatest worry kids have is not knowing what will happen to them. That's why it's important for things to be out in the open."

When Perry does something that bothers Karina, she tells him. "Although we don't always agree on every subject, at least we talk and listen to each other. Sometimes when the conversation ends, I'm still angry at Perry because I have a different opinion from his —like when he deducts a dollar from my allowance if I get in trouble. But after having said what's on my mind, I feel a little better.

"It may sound funny, but for the last year and a half— ever since Mom married Perry—I've felt as if I'm in a perfect family. All of us love and care for each other, and that's what matters most. It would be nice if we lived in a beautiful mansion with housekeepers so I wouldn't have to clean my room or do the dishes. But I wouldn't trade that for the people in this family."

Karina plans to marry someday and have children of her own. "I want at least two kids, a boy and a girl. I wouldn't want to have an only child. It would be too lonely for the kid. While I'm not sure what job I want to have when I'm older, I've got lots of time to think about that. Right now, I'm concentrating on enjoying my life."

Afterword

Love and caring, the promise of stability, and a feeling of being valued and special are important, recurrent themes in this book. They are also the basic needs of all children. Meeting these needs can sometimes be difficult when a marriage is disrupted by a divorce or a death, and parents then remarry.

Guidelines have recently emerged to help parents in this situation. These suggestions have come from stepfamily research and from the many families who have shared their experiences with such organizations as Stepfamily Association of America. Listed below are some of the insights and tactics that have helped adults in remarried households to create a home that provides children's basic needs. This environment has the additional benefit of helping young

. . . .

people cope with the changes and transitions in their lives—now and in the future.

1. At the start of a stepfamily, the expectation that love and caring occur quickly and that chaos calms rapidly is a myth. Belief in this myth can stand in the way of remarriage adjustment. Stepfamily adults need to give themselves and their children enough time and emotional space to learn about one another and for the household rules and ways of doing things to become established.

2. Relationships grow from positive shared memories and a tolerance of differences between people. It takes time for shared memories to exist, and acceptance of differences is an important aspect of these memories. When, for example, a stepparent and stepchildren can laugh together over the differences in their preferred TV programs or their tastes in food, this communicates that differences are all right. A stepparent who rejects this diversity sends an opposite message. Furthermore, acceptance of the children's tastes not only helps develop healthy, new relationships, but it also promotes the growth of the children's self-esteem.

3. Stepparents need to make opportunities to do things with their stepchildren, one at a time. It's particularly important for stepparents and stepchildren to have fun together and to share with one another aspects of their

past and present: what they like to do, what they don't like to do, and things that have meant a lot to them.

4. Stepparents need to make clear that they have special skills or ideas that are different from those of a stepchild's parent in another household or in his/her memory. Children do not like to feel that a stepparent is trying to replace their parent in another household. However, they can appreciate an additional person who cares about them and who may grow to love them and be loved by them.

5. Parents who have remarried often feel guilty that their biological children have been hurt by all the changes in their lives. In a stepfamily, everyone has experienced a number of profound losses, and anger and sadness often accompany loss. These feelings are to be expected. Parents can help by acknowledging their children's reactions to change, and when there has been enough time for children to become familiar with the changes in their new household, they can let go of the past and begin to enjoy the present. Appropriate books can be valuable, as can the chance to talk to other children in similar situations; indeed, many schools and stepfamily support organizations are beginning to offer groups for children of divorce and remarriage.

6. Children's well-being tends to be enhanced when, if possible, they are in contact with both of their bio-

logical parents. They also experience fewer feelings of loss if they have special one-on-one times with their biological parents. These moments help maintain important close relationships.

7. In a stepfamily household, the two adults need to work together to determine the rules and limits. Initially, while supporting each other, they need to let the children's biological parent enforce the limits that have been worked out. Stepparents can take on similar parenting roles when they have had the opportunity to build positive relationships with their stepchildren. By including the children in family decision-making, parents can help them feel their lives are more within their control.

8. Adults in remarried households need to plan for regular times to have fun together so that their relationship, the foundation for the unit, will grow strong. This strength will give the children a sense of present and future household stability and serve as an important model for their own future couple relationships.

The basic stepfamily task is to develop meaningful relationships among individuals who have not lived together previously. Throughout *Talking About Stepfamilies*, the young people make clear that it is not material things that create lasting relationships or foster self-esteem. It is, rather, the gift of relationships based on understanding, acceptance, and enjoyable shared time. Many stepfamily adults have found that giving this gift brings deep emotional satisfaction to parents and stepparents as well.

Dr. Emily V. Visher
cofounder, Stepfamily Association of America
coauthor, *How to Win as a Stepfamily*

Bibliography

For Children:

Berman, Claire. *What Am I Doing in a Stepfamily?* Secaucus, N.J.: Lyle Stuart, Inc., 1981.

Explores the sensitive issues children face when their parents remarry, including the myth of the mean stepmother, adjusting to stepsiblings and/or a new baby, confusion over visitation rights. Parents can benefit from this book, too.

Bradley, Buff. *Where Do I Belong? A Kids' Guide to Stepfamilies.* Reading, Mass.: Addison Wesley, 1982.

Discusses the multitude of changes children experience when they become part of a stepfamily and describes the confusion often felt in this situation.

Craven, Linda. *Stepfamilies: New Patterns of Harmony.* New York: Julian Messner, 1982.

Talks about the ways in which a stepfamily differs from a nuclear family and the problems that may arise because of this. Offers a positive approach for difficult stepfamily encounters. Lists organizations from which stepfamilies might get advice and counseling.

Gardner, Richard. *The Boys and Girls Book about Stepfamilies.* New York: Bantam Books, 1982.

Helps children in stepfamilies learn to constructively express their feelings to other family members. Answers important questions stepchildren may have about their family situations.

Krementz, Jill. *How it Feels When a Parent Dies.* New York: Knopf, 1981.

Eighteen children speak of their feelings and experiences when their mother or father has died.

For Adults:

Berman, Claire. *Making It as a Stepparent.* New York: Harper & Row, 1986.

Based on her hundreds of interviews with parents, stepparents, and professionals in the field, Berman offers information on how to make the most of a stepfamily situation.

Bernstein, Anne C., Ph.D. *Yours, Mine and Ours.* New York: Scribners' Sons, 1989.

What it's like for a child when his or her parent remarries and then has a new baby. Written by a stepparent and mother of a mutual child. Gives advice to others in the same situation.

Brooks, Andree. "For Stepfathers, Trust Comes Slowly." *The New York Times*, December 1, 1988.

Discusses the difficulties stepfathers face and why they seem to have more trouble bonding with stepdaughters than stepsons.

Capaldi, Frederick, and Barbara McRae. *Stepfamilies*. New York: Franklin Watts, 1979.

Details the feelings children are likely to experience when they become part of a stepfamily. Helps parents and stepparents to better understand their child's behavior.

Kutner, Lawrence. "In Blended Families, Rivalries Intensify." *The New York Times*, January 5, 1989.

Describes subtle changes that take place when children become part of a stepfamily, particularly when stepsiblings are involved. Sees antagonisms lessening after members have lived together more than two years.

————. "Parent and Child." *The New York Times*, April 20, 1989.

Explores how children respond to a new baby in their stepfamily and what parents and stepparents can do to ease the adjustment.

Savage, Karen, and Patricia Adams. *The Good Stepmother*. New York: Crown, 1988.

Savage, a psychotherapist and stepmother, explores the ups and downs of being a stepparent—with personal anecdotes and others' accounts.

Visher, Emily and John. *How to Win as a Stepfamily.* New York: Dembner Books, 1982.

An encouraging and helpful guide on how to succeed as a stepfamily, by the cofounders of Stepfamily Association of America. Discusses the needs of children at different ages and stages, and how parents and stepparents can make life easier for them.

Sources of Help

Alateen
Al-Anon Family Group Headquarters, Inc.
1-800-344-2666
24-hour answering service (including Alaska, Hawaii, Puerto Rico,
and Virgin Islands)
1-212-254-7230 or 7231 (New York and Canada)

Child Help's
Child Abuse Hotline USA-National
1-800-422-4453 (1-800-4-A-CHILD)

The National Association for Children of Alcoholics
Suite 201
31706 Coast Highway
South Laguna, CA 92677
1-714-499-3889

Information and referrals for therapy and treatment programs for children of alcoholics; books and organizations; local chapters; and support groups.

National Institute on Drug Abuse Helpline
1-800-843-4971

Information provided for alcohol and drug problems.

National Runaway Switchboard
1-800-621-4000

Offers help to runaways and assists them if they want to contact relatives.

National Self-Help Clearinghouse
25 West 43rd Street
New York, NY 10036

Supplies information about local self-help groups and how to start such groups.

Remarrieds, Inc.
Box 472
Santa Ana, CA 92701

Offers educational and social programs.

Stepfamily Association of America, Inc.
215 Centennial Mall South, Suite 212
Lincoln, NE 68508
1-402-477-STEP

Provides educational resources for stepfamilies and professionals. Offers a quarterly publication highlighting matters of concern for stepfamilies, as well as a current booklist and names of stepfamily support groups throughout the country.

. . . .

Stepfamily Foundation, Inc.
333 West End Avenue
New York, NY 10023

Individual and family counseling. Newsletter.

Index

· ·